REMARKABLE
CRICKET
GROUNDS

Dedication
To Andrew Ward, with many thanks

Author's Acknowledgements

I am extremely grateful for the assistance of three people in particular. Jill Haas read every word of the manuscript and improved it with many suggestions. Andrew Ward eased what was a very tight deadline with contributions about several grounds. Matthew Levison tried to explain in words of one syllable the significance and symbolism of the designs of some of the newer stadiums, although I don't think he expected me to understand what he told me and I'm not sure that I did. I was also in touch with many club officials. Although they are busy enough, my calls were always returned. They were uniformly patient with my enquiries, offering me gems of information which added much interesting detail to the book. In almost all instances they read over my draft, suggesting corrections where necessary. They are the people on whom club cricket in this country is based and they do a selfless and time-consuming job at the grass roots, sometimes literally, as a good number double up as groundsman. With apologies for any omissions, my sincere thanks to (alphabetically by club):

Bill Starr (Audley End CC)
Bill Brooke (Bamburgh Castle CC)
David Hughes (Blenheim Park CC)
Doug Sherring (Bridgetown CC)
Tony Greaves (Bude North Cornwall CC)
Patrick Lovering (Castle Ashby CC)
Nigel Dixon (Coniston CC)
Keith Richardson (Keswick CC)
Robin May (Lynton & Lynmouth CC)
Jonathan Campion (Mezica CC)
Julia Gault (Mitcham CC)
Steve Caygill, Peter Jackson (Raby Castle CC)
John Hallam, Alex McKay and John Zani (St Moritz CC)
Elizabeth Skinner and Paul Grellier (Sheepscombe CC)
Martin Darlow (Southill Park CC)
Harry Mead (Spout House CC)
David Wildgoose (Stoneleigh Abbey CC)
Franklin Barrett and Elizabeth Wells (Westminster School)

My need for help and information also brought me into contact with Mike Amos of the *Northern Echo*, John Barclay of Sussex CCC and Derek Barnard, former Chairman of the Cricket Society, and very many thanks to them.

Photo Credits

All photos courtesy of Getty Images with the exception of the following:
Alamy: 4, 12, 13, 19, 24-25, 30-31, 32, 33, 40, 41, 48, 49, 56, 57, 79, 84, 85 (left), 100, 112,114-115, 116, 117 (right), 119 (top + left), 130, 139, 152 (top + middle). Jill Mead: 7, 140, 141, 142, 143. Richard Woods: 11 (bottom left). Rambling Man 11 (bottom left). Mark A. Roberts: 22-23. Frank Hopkinson: 28, 29, 102, 103. WCIB Media: 51 (top). Timohty Barton: 51 (bottom). Corbis-Getty: 53, 87, 98 (bottom), 104, 105, 116 (bottom), 132 (bottom), 148-149, 153. Skyepics: 66. Califlier001: 69. Goran Janson: 94 (top), 95. Marilyn Peddle: 101 (bottom). Phil Draper (www.churchwarden.com): 101 (top). Paul Snook 106, 107. Paul Brassington. 108-109. Bill Lowis: 109 (bottom). Helen Devereux: 122 (right). Liz O'Sullivan: 128. Jonathan Campion (JonathanCampion.com): 146, 147. Anthony Burt: 158-159.

First published in the United Kingdom in 2021 by Pavilion Books
43 Great Ormond Street, London WC1N 3HZ

This book is a shortened, revised version of *Remarkable Cricket Grounds* - Copyright © Pavilion Books Company Ltd, 2016

ISBN 978-1-911663-84-3

A CIP catalogue record for this book is available from the British Library.
Reproduction by Rival UK
Printed and bound by Toppan Leefung, China
Front cover photo: Coniston CC (Alamy)
Back cover photos, top to bottom: Blenheim Palace (Alamy), Lord's (Getty), Valley of the Rocks, (Alamy), Dharamshala (Getty).

About the Author

Brian Levison has a lifelong interest in cricket and played club cricket for several years. His books include the highly acclaimed cricket anthology *All in a Day's Play* (2012), *Amazing & Extraordinary Facts: Cricket* (2012). He is the author of the large format version of *Remarkable Cricket Grounds* which was shortlisted for Illustrated Sports Book of the Year in 2017, and also the companion title, *Remarkable Village Cricket Grounds* (2018).

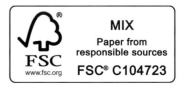

REMARKABLE CRICKET GROUNDS

— BRIAN LEVISON —

PAVILION

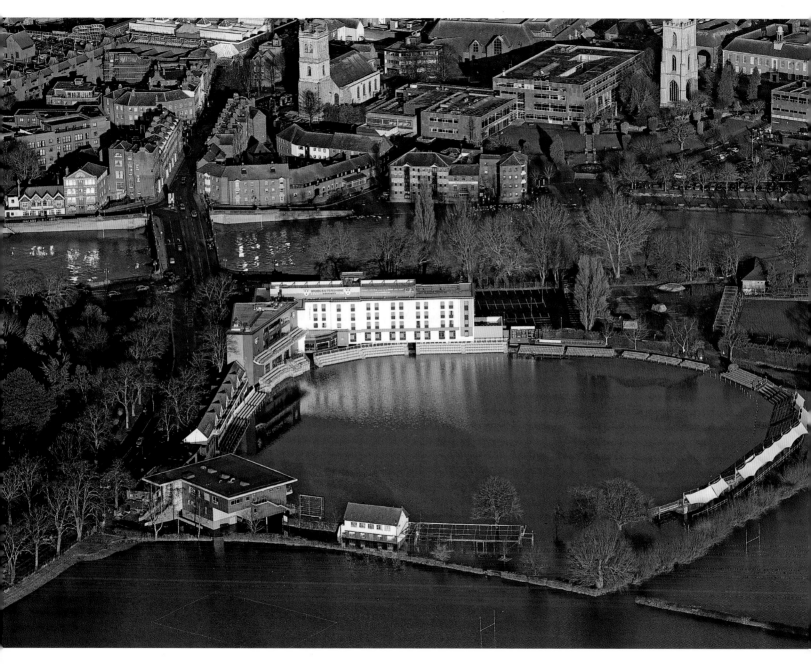

Introduction

Opened in 1896, the New Road cricket ground in Worcester arrived too late for the young Edward Elgar to have bunked off and watched a game of cricket on his way from Broadheath to the music library at Worcester Cathedral. Standing high on the banks of the River Severn, one of the finest views of the soaring Gothic structure is from across the river at the cricket ground, and when the life of England's greatest composer was celebrated with his portrait on a £20 note, it was accompanied by a view of the cathedral from just about where the New Road square would be.

Apart from being the only cricket ground view on a banknote, New Road is also remarkable as one of the most regularly flooded first-class cricket venues in the world. The Severn consistently bursts its banks in winter and covers the ground with a fine layer of silt. The groundsmen have developed a regime to cope; it's only when the floods come in July, as they did in 2007, that all hell breaks loose.

As author Brian Levison discovered, a similar fate befell Keswick Cricket Club and their ground at Fitz Park after Storm Desmond

LEFT: New Road and the neighbouring Kings School cricket pitches in Worcester are regularly flooded over winter, as this picture from December 2013 demonstrates. It's when the Severn receives an unseasonal deluge in July that major disruption occurs.

RIGHT: Newlands Cricket Ground, Cape Town.

deluged the Lake District in December 2015. The river Greta overflowed, flooding the ground for the very first time and depositing 700 tonnes of silt onto the site.

Fitz Park is one of many remarkable cricket grounds included in this collection of astonishing places where cricket is played. The criteria for inclusion are manyfold, with a touch of the Guinness Book of Records to some of them, such as the highest, oldest or largest cricket grounds. The military school at Chail in Himachal Pradesh, India, reckons to have the highest cricket ground in the world. Chail is a hill station not far from Shimla where the British spent their summers getting away from the infernal heat. It's in

the same province as another remarkable ground, the Himachal Pradesh Cricket Association Stadium at Dharamshala. The Himalayas form a snow-capped backdrop to cricket at this venue, with its multi-coloured stands, that hosted games in the 2016 Twenty20 World Cup.

Across the border in Pakistan, in Pakistan-administered Kashmir, there is Narol, a cricket ground still recovering from the devastating 2005 earthquake. During the emergency, the outfield was used to land helicopters as part of the relief effort, and it subsequently fell into disrepair as sport took a backseat to the necessities of life. Like the region of Azad Kashmir, it is on the road to

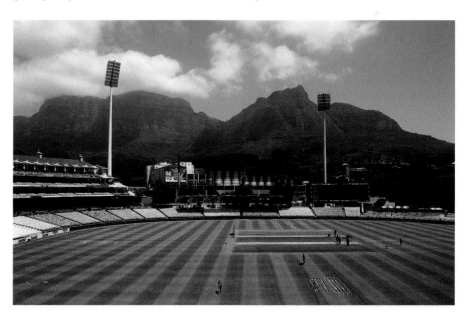

recovery with help from the Pakistan Cricket Board.

We have sought out cricket played (regularly) in unexpected places, along with some of the pioneering efforts to establish cricket in new territories where the sound of leather against ash is preferred to leather against willow. Above all we have searched for some of the most breathtakingly beautiful places where the game is played.

Beauty, as we are often reminded, is in the eye of the beholder, but for lifelong fans of the Oval, beauty has been in the retention of the gas holders. An object of industrial necessity, when they were first erected in 1853 members of Surrey CCC wrote to *The Times* at the sheer effrontery of such an imposition. Now they are seen as an object of both industrial history and beauty and their Grade II listing in March 2016 has meant they have a fair old innings to come.

A more conventional beauty is presented by the many thatched pavilions on English cricket grounds. Bridgetown Cricket Ground in Somerset has one, but the Whitbread Estate in Bedfordshire trumps that with a separate thatched scoreboard. In the past, *Wisden* and the *Daily Telegraph* have run competitions to find the most beautiful village cricket grounds and a few of these serial beauty contestants have made it through once again. Fitz Park in Keswick and Coniston Cricket Club both have the majestic backdrop of the Lake District to be photographed against from one side of the ground. However, Lynton and Lynmouth CC's ground in the Valley of the Rocks, North Devon, presents a real predicament to photographers. It can yield spectacular photographs viewed from the east, west,

north and south, it all depends on how much climbing they are prepared to do.

There are some remarkable cricket grounds that wouldn't necessarily make it onto a postcard. The Charters Towers pitches in Queensland are unlikely to feature in polls for the most picturesque, but the Goldfield Ashes tournament is remarkable in that it attracts 200 teams from around the world for what's billed as the biggest cricket festival in the Southern Hemisphere. It would be natural to assume that this festival is held in a big urban centre like Melbourne or a popular tourist destination, but Charters Towers is a former goldmining town of 8,000 souls on the Flinders Highway, a 14-hour drive from Brisbane.

There are a couple of cricket pitches now established in a Berlin arena that was regularly featured in newsreels from the 1930s. The Maifeld, bordering the Olympic stadium, was used to host the polo, dressage events and also the finish of the marathon at the 1936 Olympic Games. On a more sinister note, it also hosted vast Nazi rallies including joint addresses by Hitler and Mussolini in 1937. In the post-war partition of Berlin it ended up in the British sector, so also has happier memories of Queen Elizabeth II reviewing the troops stationed there. Now it is home to Berlin Cricket Club.

Elsewhere in this alphabetically ordered book, established Test grounds sit cheek by jowl with pitches in Slovenia, Corfu and St Moritz.

So much can depend on chance in cricket and there are some beautiful grounds that by the editorial toss of a coin didn't quite make it into the book. Cockington near Torquay in

Devon is a beautiful setting, while Patterdale in the Ullswater valley rivals Keswick and Coniston for Lake District splendour. The pitches at Malvern College have the glorious backdrop of the Malvern Hills, while playing in the shadow of Arthur's Seat, Morton Cricket Club's ground, the Meadows, is one of the most picturesque in Scotland.

Some of the sites, such as Spout House in Yorkshire, are simply remarkable in that they have kept a traditional cricket team going for 150 years, despite the difficulties of getting a side out in remote rural areas. Lack of players is now threatening this remarkable club. Jill Mead's photographs of the club's sheep field games wonderfully illustrate that where there is a will, there can be a game. Within such a glorious setting, and with such a heritage to the event, the old saying can be trotted out and truly meant: it's not about the winning, it is about the taking part. In 2021, with the country recovering from the devastation of Covid, supporting cricket clubs has never been more important.

Frank Hopkinson,
Editor

RIGHT: The traditional slow outfield at Spout House near Bilsdale, North Yorkshire, under threat from a lack of players.

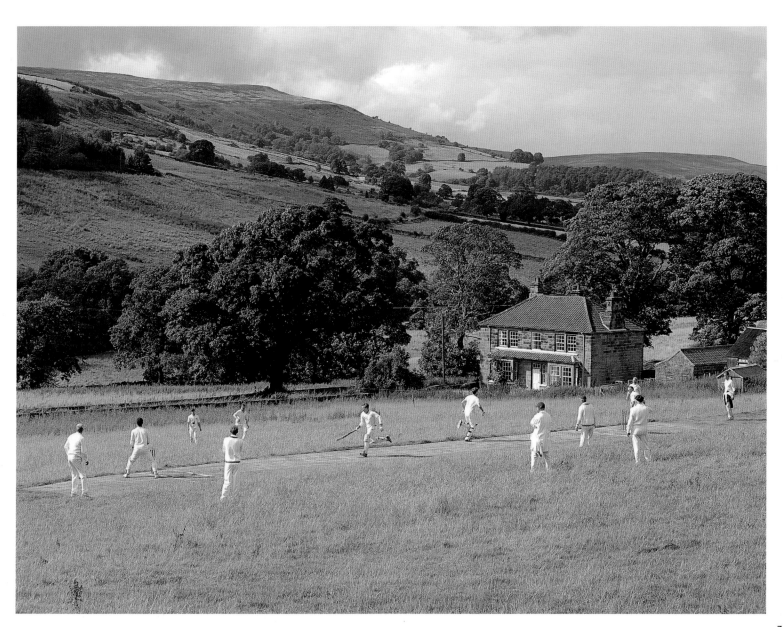

Adelaide Oval

Adelaide, South Australia

Adelaide Oval has witnessed some of the most resonant moments in Test cricket, although not all the drama has been on the field. From 2009 to 2013, the ground underwent a massive, highly controversial redevelopment.

The Oval dates back to 1871, with first-class cricket beginning in 1877 and Test cricket in 1884 against England. Famous incidents include the Fourth Test of the infamous Bodyline Series in 1932–33. The English fast bowler Harold Larwood, bowling at his fiercest, struck and injured the Australian batsmen Bill Woodfull and Bert Oldfield. Diplomatic relations between the two countries became very strained. In 1993, the West Indies won an exciting Test by one run, and in the 1995 Boxing Day Test, umpire Darrell Hair notoriously no-balled the Sri Lankan off-spinner Muttiah Muralitharan for throwing. More recently, the first-ever day-night Test with pink ball took place here in 2015.

The ground has always been held in affectionate regard because of its many traditional features. At the north end is the famous hand-operated scoreboard dating back to 1911, which sits beside the landscaped Northern Mound. Behind it is a beautiful copse of full-leaved Moreton Bay fig trees, ironically planted originally to block the view of non-paying spectators. St Peter's Cathedral rises in the background. Stands were dedicated to the state's most famous cricketers, such as Sir Donald Bradman, the Chappell brothers and George Giffen.

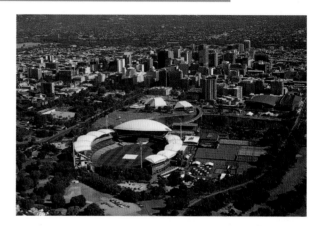

Ground development never stood still in all these years, but cricket is by no means the only popular sport in South Australia. Pressure was building for a new Aussie Rules venue. But the state saw no point in such a costly new venture, when it might be possible to integrate the two sports in one resource, the Adelaide Oval.

To do this, a way had to be found to preserve as many of the Heritage Status features as possible. Particularly important were the Northern Mound, the scoreboard, the fig trees and the view beyond the stadium. The initial plans drew objections and threats of delisting from the National Trust of South Australia. Eventually, after a struggle, the most important items were protected from the bulldozers, although the scoreboard is now supplemented by a new video screen. The famous names of the old stands have been replaced by the prosaic Western, Eastern and Riverbank stands.

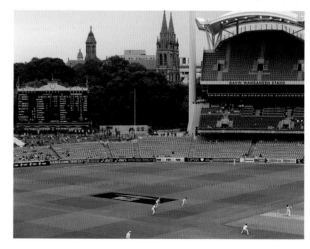

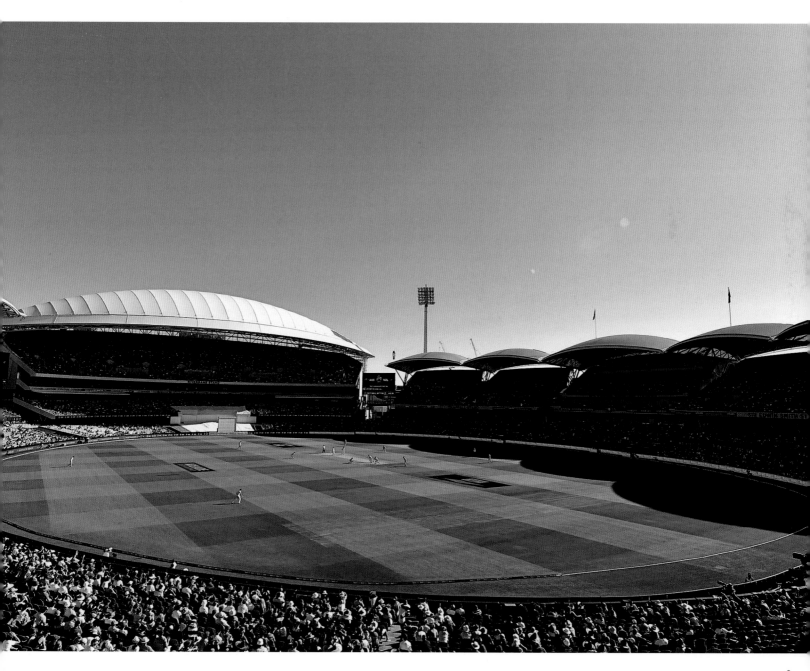

Along the way, the redesigned Oval has changed its dimensions to accommodate Aussie Rules and increased its ground capacity from 34,000 to over 53,000. Football spelt the end for a traditional home-grown pitch and Test matches since 2013 have been played on drop-in pitches. The old Adelaide pitches were reckoned to be the best batting wicket in Australia and in November 2019 David Warner revived those memories when he scored 335, the highest-ever individual Test score at the ground, against Pakistan.

The redevelopment was completed in 2014 at a cost of A\$535 million. Not everyone was happy. The Kaurna, the original people of the Adelaide Plains, still have unrecognised

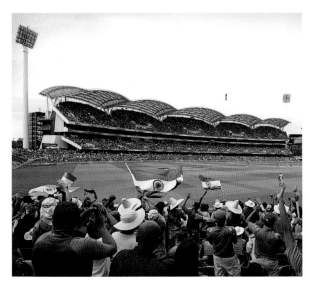

territorial claims. Some spectators say that stands block out views to the hills and that they cast earlier and larger shadows across the ground. Journalist Christian Ryan complains that in two thirds of the seats round the ground you can no longer see the cathedral and when you can, it is often just the tips of two spires. And you can't run fives any more...

But local traders point out the improved access to the Adelaide shops and compare match days to high-spending New Year's Eve. Others look at the fig trees and the old scoreboard and think an acceptable compromise has been achieved.

Home to: West End Redbacks

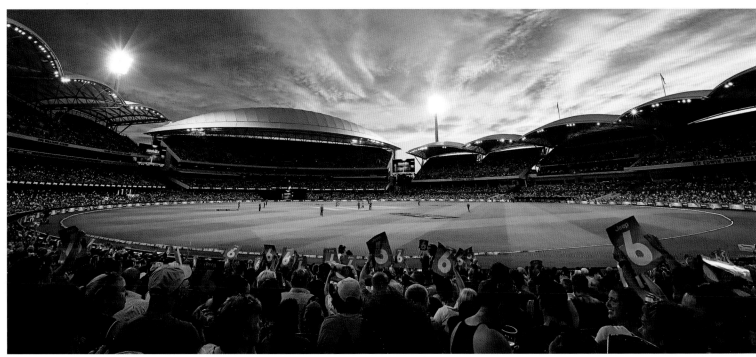

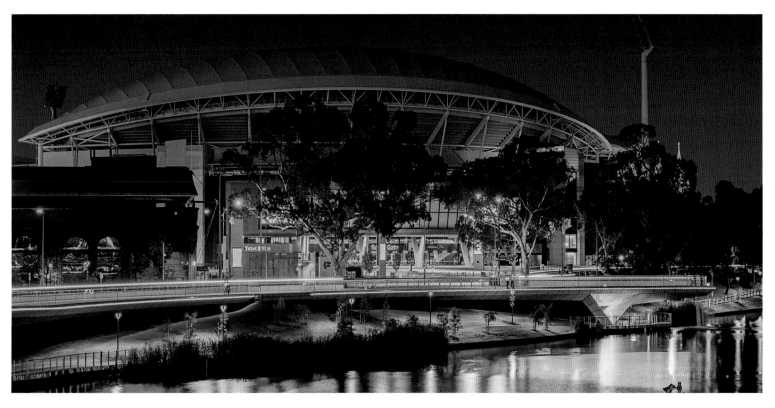

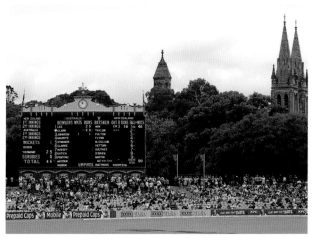

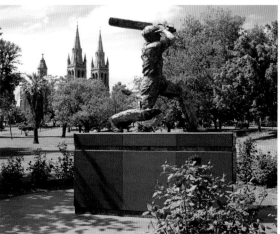

FAR LEFT: The hand-operated scoreboard was installed in 1911. The clock was added in 1912 and the wind vane in the 1930s.

LEFT: A statue of Sir Donald Bradman, acknowledged as the greatest batsman of all time. Bradman made his first-class debut at the Adelaide Oval aged 19.

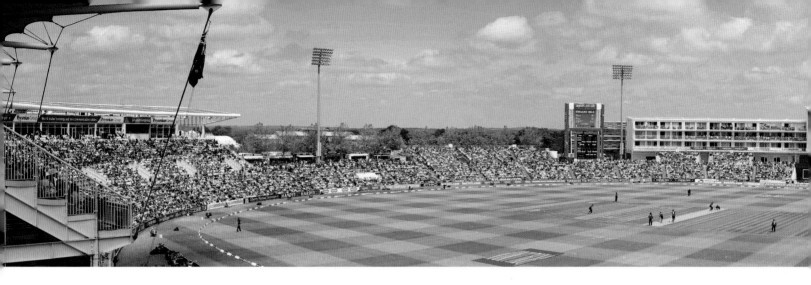

Ageas Bowl

West End, Hampshire, England

On 4 May 2001, a one-day game was played between Hampshire and Surrey at that rarest of things, a completely new county venue. It was not the upgrade of an existing pitch but the creation from scratch of a new Test-standard cricket ground. The construction of Hampshire's new home, the Rose Bowl (known as the Ageas Bowl after its sponsors), must rank as one of the most breathtakingly ambitious undertakings in recent English cricket history.

To take what was basically a green-field site on the side of a gently sloping meadow in the middle of the countryside (though with access to a motorway) and convert it into the sophisticated cricket complex it now is, required nerve, imagination and a lot of money. The architecture is modern and exciting. The tented roof of the pavilion may bring the Mound Stand at Lord's to mind

and indeed Sir Michael Hopkins designed both structures. Overlooking the ground is a Hilton Hotel from whose bedroom balconies there is a good view of the cricket. A touching reminder of Hampshire greats is the naming of one of the roads, Marshall Drive, after the great West Indian players, Roy and Malcolm Marshall. In the 1950s and 60s, a loudspeaker van used to tour Southsea front to alert day-trippers that Roy Marshall, a very aggressive and entertaining opener, was batting. But potential spectators had to hurry as Marshall was not renowned for long stays at the crease. Hampshire heroes such as Gordon Greenidge, Derek Shackleton, Barry Richards and Shane Warne are also not forgotten.

The driving force behind this achievement has been Hampshire's chairman, Rod Bransgrove. The award of Tests against Sri

Lanka (2011) and India (2014) met his goal of creating a Test-class facility, but it is no secret that his great ambition is to welcome an Ashes Test. Along the way there have certainly been problems. In 2012, financial issues resulted in the sale of the ground to the local council.

During the summer of 2020 the ground was one of only two bio-secure Test venues – the other was Old Trafford – used for the 'last-minute' tours by the West Indies, Pakistan and Ireland. A mixture of Tests, ODIs and Twenty20 games were played. Both grounds were chosen because of their integrated (Hilton) hotel facilities and the great irony was that rain, so commonly attributed to Manchester, often fell on the Ageas Bowl, while Old Trafford remained gloriously sunny.

Home to: Hampshire County Cricket Club

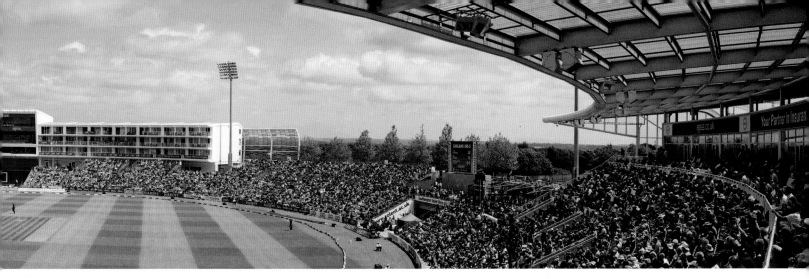

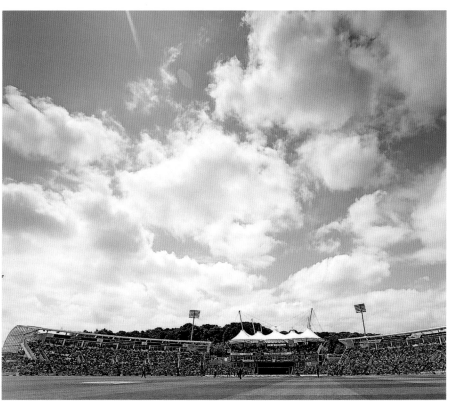

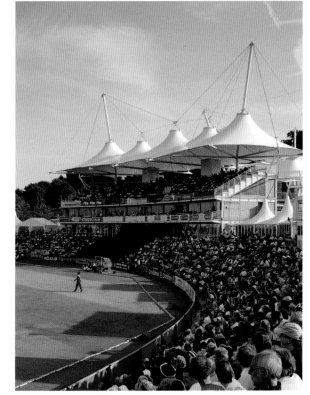

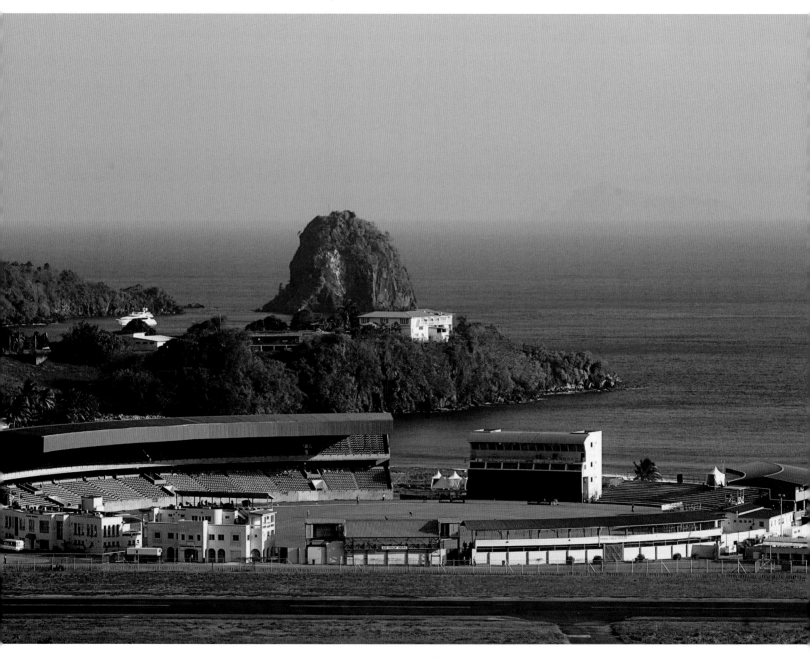

Arnos Vale Stadium

Kingstown, Saint Vincent, Windward Islands

Arnos Vale is better known locally as the Playing Fields and has been hosting international games since 1981. It is not a regular West Indies Test venue, but has seen its fair share of ODI games in which the West Indies normally do well, having won 18 and tied one out of 23 played. A major refurbishment costing EC (East Caribbean) $20 million took place in preparation for the 2007 World Cup, though only warm-up games were played here.

The ground is frequently to be found on lists of the 10 most beautiful venues. *GQ* magazine said the stadium 'almost looks like a postcard from the Caribbean – on the edge of the ocean, so you might be able to actually watch the action from a luxury yacht and with green tropical cliffs in the vicinity.' Saint Vincent was Captain Bligh's original destination before the mutiny on the *Bounty* detained him. When he finally arrived he brought with him a breadfruit tree whose descendants still grow here today. Fans of the *Pirates of the Caribbean* films may recognise locations where the film was shot.

Less heroically, Arnos Vale was the scene of one of the West Indies most humiliating defeats in recent years when Bangladesh beat them by 95 runs in 2009. The regular Test team, captained by Chris Gayle, refused to play due to a contractual dispute with the West Indies Cricket Board and was replaced by a team totalling only 22 caps. Of the seven debutants in the West Indies side, only Kemar Roach went on to have an extensive Test career. The home side was almost saved by the hurricane season which restricted play and the game could easily have been rained off. Ironically, drainage installed for the 2007 World Cup proved so efficient that enough play was possible for a Bangladesh victory.

Home to: Windward Islands

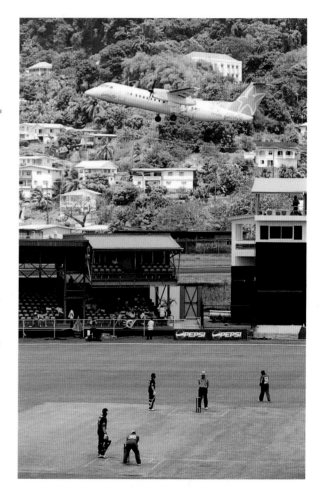

RIGHT: The aptly named Airport End. The stadium is adjacent to E.T. Joshua Airport.

Bamburgh Castle

Northumberland, England

Perched high above the North Sea on the coast of Northumberland, the magnificent Bamburgh Castle has a long·and turbulent history. Originally a royal castle established in Anglo-Saxon times, it has been ransacked by the Vikings and fought over in the Wars of the Roses. Royal visitors included William II, Edward I and Henry VI, though usually not in peaceful circumstances. A glance at its massive dimensions makes it easy to understand why James I decided the castle was too expensive to maintain and in 1610 it was sold into private hands. Over the centuries that have passed since then, the castle regularly thrived and fell into disrepair. Lord Armstrong (1810–1900), an inventor and engineer, finally stabilised its fortunes just before his death. The castle still remains in the hands of the Armstrong family and its current owner, Francis Watson-Armstrong, is the cricket club's president. It is a popular location for films and scenes from *Becket*, *The Devils*, *Elizabeth* and two versions of *Macbeth*, among others, were shot here.

Founded in 1860, the club was first based on the Glebe Field in Bamburgh but moved to Castle Green in 1895, after Lord Armstrong landscaped the area. In a friendly arrangement it does not pay rent but instead cuts the green twice a week, even during the football season. If photographs seem to show the cricket as an isolated activity, beyond the lens many knock-up games are taking place, as well as croquet just outside the boundary. Every so often a hit from the cricket will land on the greens, no doubt prompting a little light banter.

J.M.W. Turner painted the castle veiled by sea spray, capturing a wild, romantic side in an image which has been called 'one of the finest watercolour drawings in the world'. Playing in its shadow can be distracting to visiting sides who sometimes goggle at the castle when they should be assessing the home team's bowling. Even Prudhoe CC, with its own castle to be proud of, is happy to pose in front of Bamburgh Castle's mighty edifice for a team photograph. Local weather conditions ensure that sight screens are dispensed with because they are likely to get blown over, and once in a while play comes to a halt due to sea fret (fog).

Echoes of the past are recalled when St Cuthbert's, named after a local saint, are the visitors and the ground is annually invaded by Vikings – the Northumberland Vikings CC, that is.

Home to: Bamburgh Castle Cricket Club

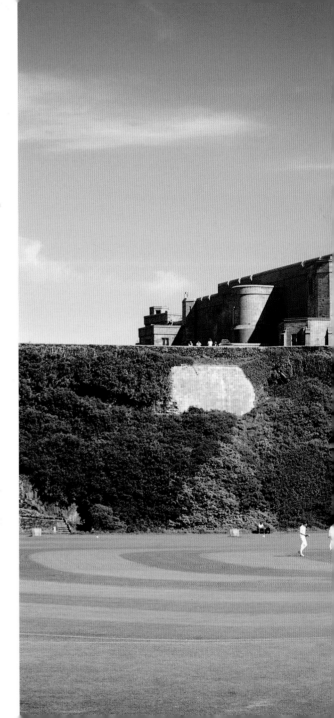

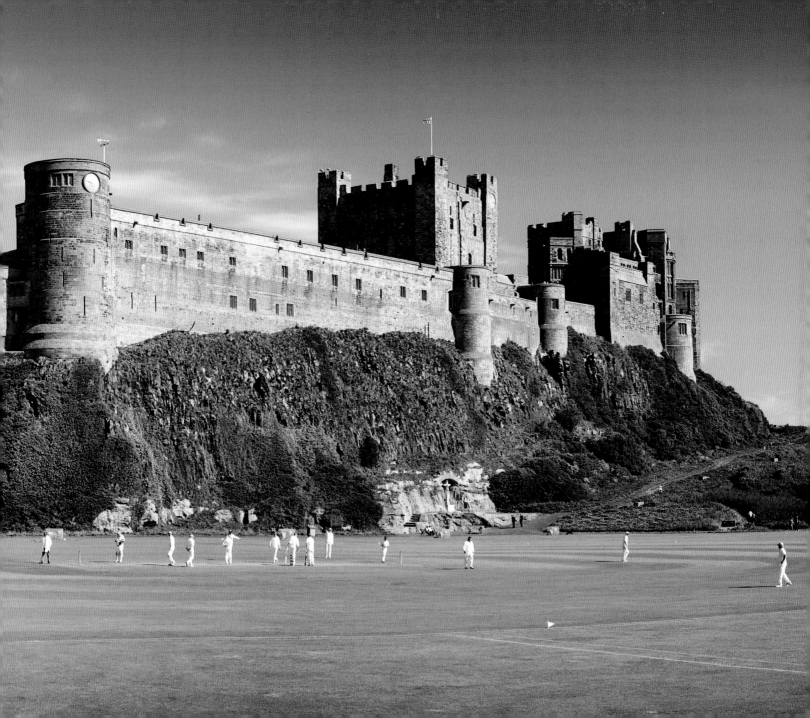

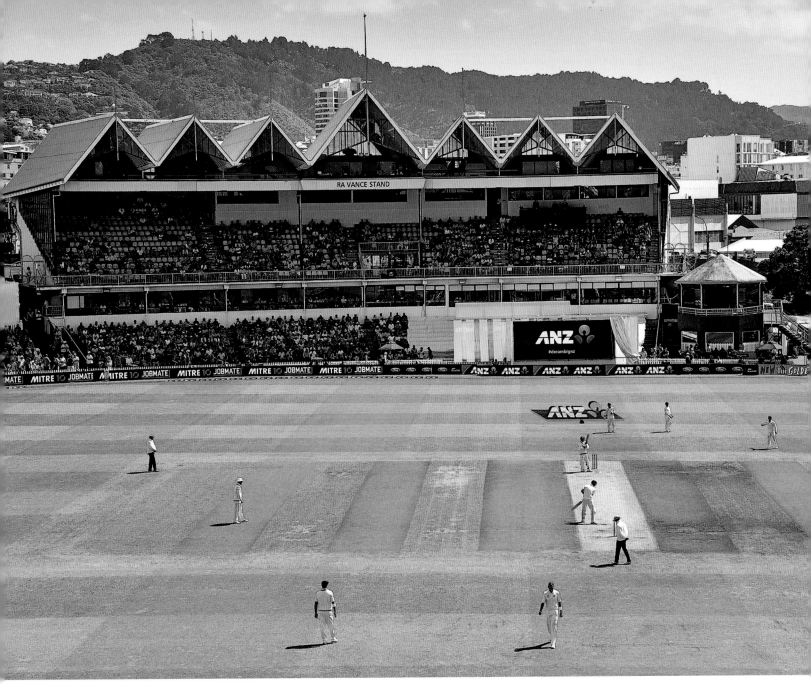

Basin Reserve

Wellington, New Zealand

Unsurprisingly, earthquakes are generally bad news for cricket arenas, causing massive damage to grounds such as the Narol Cricket Ground in Pakistan and the Hagley Oval in Christchurch, New Zealand. But in the case of the Basin Reserve, an earthquake actually created the ground.

Prior to 1855, the area was a lagoon, known as the Basin or Dock Reserve, and plans were in hand to link it to the Cook Strait by a canal. But on 23 January 1855, an earthquake of 8.2 magnitude struck, the most powerful in New Zealand's history. When it was over, Wellington's landscape had substantially changed. The area of the Basin Reserve was raised by 2 metres (6.6 feet) and became a swamp. The plans for a canal were abandoned; instead, pressure mounted to use the area for recreational facilities, in particular cricket, before it could be set aside for housing. Permission was granted in 1857, though it wasn't till 1863 that the draining of the land began, using prison labour. In 1866, the Basin Reserve was officially established

as Wellington's home of cricket and in 1868 the first match took place. A local side, the Wellington Volunteers, played a team from the visiting HMS *Falcon*. The visitors won by one wicket, though after the game an umpire apologised for the stones and thistles in the grass which had injured some of the players.

The first first-class game took place in 1873, followed by an international match in 1877. In 1925, a new grandstand, now called the Old Grandstand, was erected, which today houses a reference library and the New Zealand Cricket Museum. Among many interesting items, it contains W.G. Grace memorabilia, a Dennis Lillee aluminium bat, a Clarrie Grimmett blazer and the Addington bat of 1743, the third oldest bat in existence. In 2015 the museum mounted a special exhibition to honour the 100th Anniversary of W.G.'s death.

In 1998 the Basin Reserve was awarded Historic Place status as the oldest first-class venue in New Zealand. Once described as 'New Zealand's largest traffic island',

renovation and a little relocation has much improved the ground over the years, and, according to the *Dominion Post* in 1999, converted it 'from a rectangle to an oval, from a duckling to a swan.'

Since its first Test in 1930, the ground has hosted well over 50 Test matches and has seen many memorable feats. Sir Richard Hadlee took his 300th Test wicket here, and, in 1991, Martin Crowe and Andrew Jones put on a then-world-record partnership of 467 against Sri Lanka. Crowe's score of 299 was the highest by a New Zealander till Brendon McCullum scored 302 in February 2014, also at the Basin Reserve.

Home to: Wellington Firebirds

BELOW: The R. A. Vance stand at right and the Museum Stand beyond. With 994 seats, the Museum Stand had been closed for 8 years after being declared an earthquake risk. It was reopened in February 2020 for the Test between New Zealand and India after strengthening and redesign.

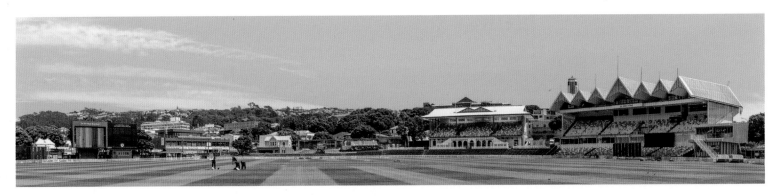

Blackfinch New Road

Worcester, England

In certain moods, New Road cricket ground, home of Worcestershire County Cricket Club, is one of the most beautiful grounds in the country. With the River Severn flowing placidly just beyond the boundary fence and overlooked by the magnificent Worcester Cathedral, on one of the better summer days New Road presents an image of England straight out of the guide books.

But both river and cathedral influence the cricket. The Severn regularly overflows its banks in the early part of the year, causing devastating flooding of the ground. With over 150 floods in the history of the club, Worcestershire accept the misfortune with a resigned shrug and hope for a couple of weeks of fine weather to get back to normal, although in June 2007 (as seen right) the impact was so bad that the club was unable to play there for the rest of the season. A rowing boat was said to be an essential item of the groundsman's equipment in the past.

The cathedral, which incorporates almost every English architectural style from Norman to Perpendicular Gothic, was the unwitting cause of a very funny incident when the excellent Gloucestershire off-spinner and wonderful cricket character Bryan 'Bomber' Wells was playing there in the 1950s. Bomber bowled off the shortest run imaginable and made the great Shane Warne's seem recklessly over-energetic. At the start of an over he saw that the cathedral clock was about to strike midday. Impishly, he decided to try and complete the over before the clock had finished chiming. With the connivance of the batsman, who patted each ball back to him, half a minute later it was finished and the clock was still striking. His captain was not best pleased and he was dropped for the next two games.

The view of the cathedral from the cricket ground is perhaps unique, as it is the only view-from-a cricket-ground to make it onto a bank note.

The £20 note issued by the Bank of England between 1999 and 2007 featured a portrait of Sir Edward Elgar and a view of the west façade of his beloved cathedral, drawn from a position that would place the artist in the New Road pavilion. If you are unfortunate enough to encounter a rainy day at the County Ground, then 5 kilometres (3 miles) away in Lower Broadheath is Elgar's birthplace, now a museum and visitor centre for one of England's most famous composers.

Home to: Worcestershire County Cricket Club

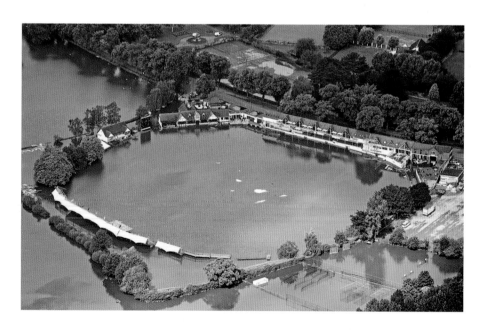

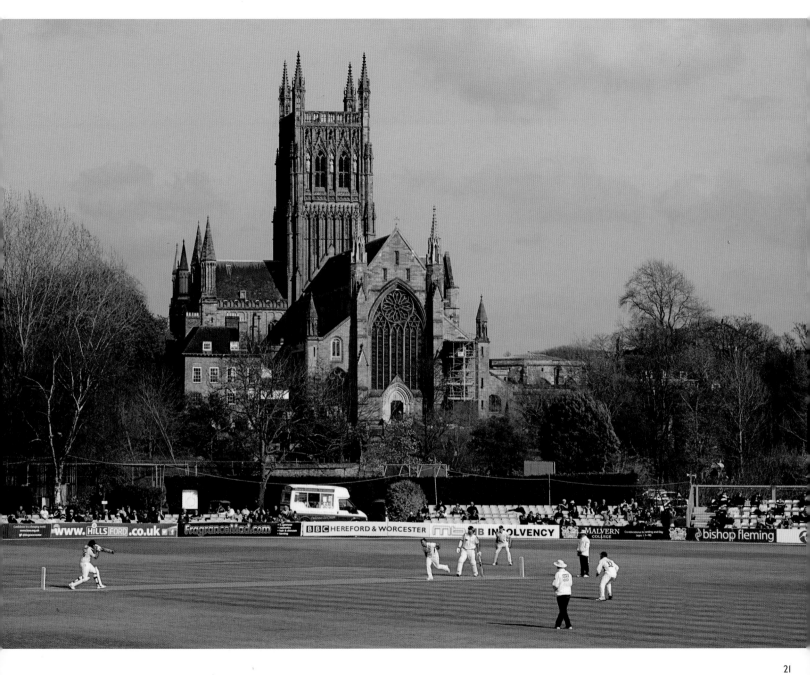

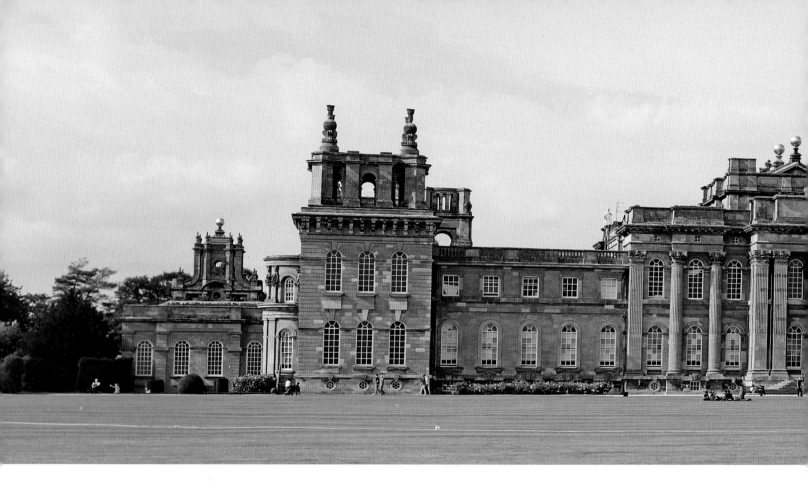

Blenheim Palace

Woodstock, Oxfordshire, England

Cricket has been played at Blenheim, home of the Dukes of Marlborough, from around the end of the 19th century. Like many other large, landed estates, Blenheim Palace ran its own team, even employing a cricket professional to ensure standards were maintained.

Regular cricket ceased once estates were no longer able to maintain a pool of cricket-playing staff and matches didn't resume till the 1950s, when the 10th Duke of Marlborough suggested that a local team be formed and offered the palace grounds as its home.

Since then, Blenheim Park Cricket Club, mainly composed of locals who live and work in the Woodstock area, has gratefully enjoyed playing on the South Lawn, and is in its own way a modest tourist attraction. The club doesn't belong to a league, but doesn't really need to. Most of its games

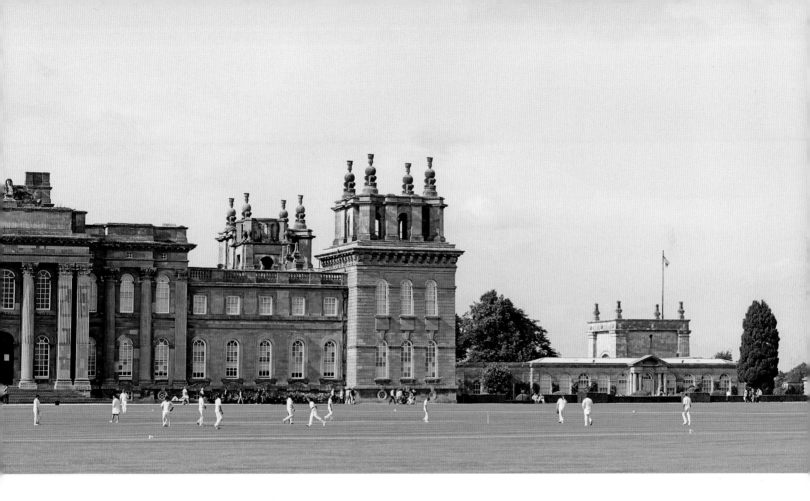

are at home because there is no shortage of teams eager to play at these beautiful and historic surroundings, conscious that Sir Winston Churchill is buried close by at Bladon. Regular visitors are I Zingari and the Bunburys, often with Ian Botham and Mark Ramprakash among the team. The club saves away games for days when the palace uses the ground itself, for example during the International Horse Trials or when it hosts its own games, such as the Commonwealth Secretariat v. the Foreign Office. The club

built its own pavilion – whose modest facilities include changing rooms but no showers – and happily makes it available to the palace as a small thank-you for the privilege of playing in such an extraordinary setting. In a cordial arrangement, the palace, which doesn't charge for use of the ground, looks after the outfield but the club prepares the wicket.

With Blenheim a popular tourist destination, the cricket sometimes has to stop so that a

visitor from a non-cricket-playing nation, who has unwittingly wandered on to the playing area, can be gently redirected. Occasionally, a 'time out' is called while a helicopter lands bringing a guest of the Duke's. It is rumoured that if you hit the palace about 100 metres (328 feet) away, you will get a reward, though this might well equal the bill for the repairs.

Home to: Blenheim Park Cricket Club

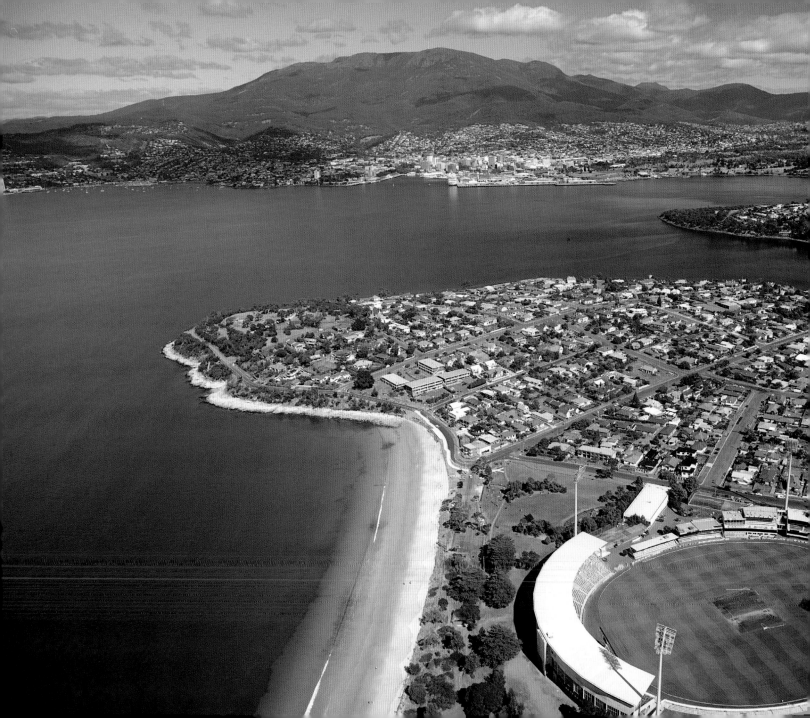

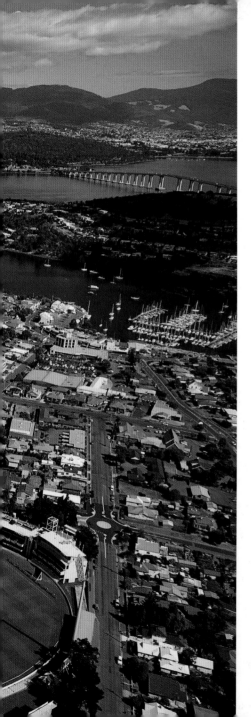

Blundstone Arena

Hobart, Tasmania, Australia

Flanked by the River Derwent and dominated by the towering heights of Mount Wellington, the Blundstone Arena, also known as Bellerive Oval, is a magnificent contemporary stadium. It was developed through a well-planned and executed strategy which has transformed cricket in Tasmania in the last 30 years or so.

Tasmania's cricket history goes back a very long way, starting at the time of the European settlement in 1803. Records show that cricket was played as early as 1806 and club cricket was well-established by the 1830s. But, bizarrely, matches often took place in June and July, in the middle of the harsh Tasmanian winter, because it reminded the homesick British settlers of the cricket that was being played in England at the same time.

Tasmania took part in the first ever first-class game in Australia, a 'timeless' match against Victoria at Launceston in 1851, played in front of 2,500 spectators. In the event, it only lasted two days, with Tasmania winning a low-scoring game by three wickets. But generally, its progress in mainstream Australian cricket proceeded by fits and starts. The state would play the odd first-class game against Victoria, perhaps not do very well, especially when faced by the new-fangled round-arm bowling, and be refused further matches. The establishment of the TCA (Tasmania Cricket Association) ground in 1880 took things a step further, but the ground had obvious shortcomings due to its location on a hill and exposure to

the winds from Mount Wellington. In 1977, after many years of trying and under the captaincy of the old Lancashire spinner, Jack Simmons, Tasmania was finally admitted to the Sheffield Shield, convincing the administrators that a new ground had to be found if Tasmanian cricket was to flourish.

The Bellerive Oval, in a suburb on the eastern shore of Hobart, was selected from a shortlist of three. At the time, it was in poor shape, having hardly changed from its early days as a recreation ground in 1914. A hump in the centre of the playing area meant that only the top half of players could be seen from the other side of the ground. Facilities were very limited with a shed serving as a pavilion and only a concrete pitch for the junior teams. But helped by substantial funding of A$2.2 million for a new grandstand, pavilion and the levelling of the field – the goose became a swan. Constant redevelopment and investment has increased the crowd capacity to 20,000.

The results are self-evident. Tasmania won the Sheffield Shield three times in 2006-7, 2010-11, and 2012-13 and the limited-overs trophy on four occasions. It has produced cricketers of the calibre of Ricky Ponting and David Boon, both of whom have stands named after them. The ground has hosted ODIs since 1988 and Tests since 1989 and although not yet on the circuit of Ashes grounds, it might well happen.

Home to: Tasmanian Tigers; Hobart Hurricanes

Boland Bank Park

Paarl, Western Cape, South Africa

Boland, meaning 'land above' or 'top country' in Afrikaans, is a region in the Western Cape Province about 60 kilometres (37 miles) east of Cape Town. The nearest large town is Paarl with a population of about 200,000. The area is famous for the variety and flavour of its wines, which have been blended in five distinct local climatic areas for more than 350 years.

Boland Park is overlooked by the dramatic Boland mountain complex which is part of a UNESCO World Heritage Site. The range contains many dramatic peaks, the highest rising to nearly 2,000 metres (6,560 feet). The catchment area comprises only 9 per cent of the Western Cape land, yet provides 60 per cent of its water. The park's picturesque setting offers spectators the shade of trees and lovely grassed embankments to relax on while watching a match. The stadium, which has a capacity of 10,000, is mainly a cricket venue but also a centre for rugby and soccer.

Boland cricket team has made steady progress since 1992 when it was playing B-grade cricket. Bob Woolmer, the former England Test player, was then appointed coach and by 1994 the province had attained A-status, although at this point Woolmer left to become coach of the national team. Since then, the team has played first-class cricket in its own right in the Provincial Three-Day Challenge.

A number of ODIs have been played at the ground, including three matches in the 2003 World Cup, but not any Tests or Twenty20 internationals as yet. The first ODI to be played here in 1997 between India and Zimbabwe proved to be a cliff-hanger that has not been matched since. The sides included players like Ganguly, Tendulkar, Dravid, Andy Flower and Heath Streak. Zimbabwe scored 236 and the scores were level with two balls to go when Robin Singh on 48 was run out going for the winning run, making the match a tie.

Home to: Boland cricket team, Cape Cobras, Paarl Rocks (Mzansi Super League)

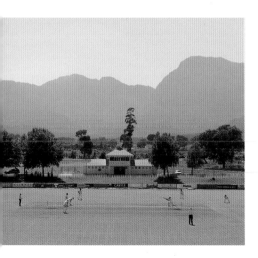

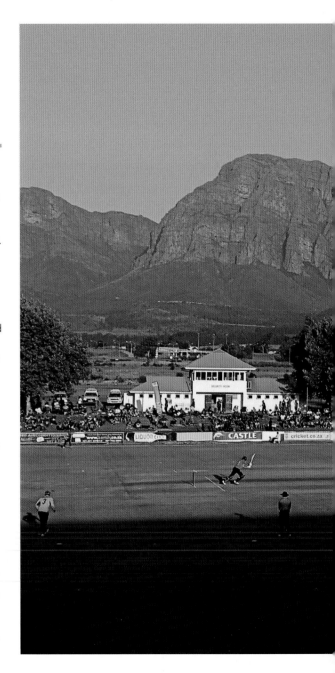

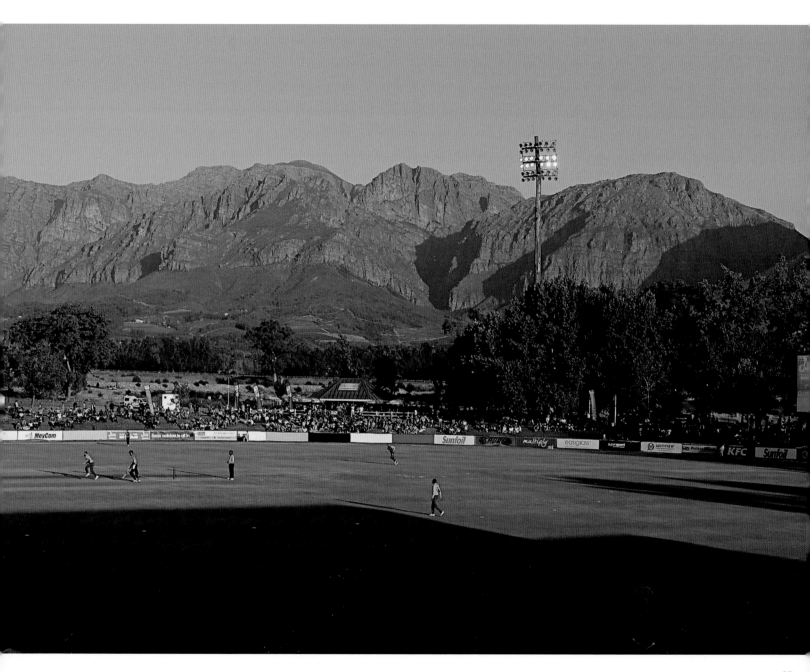

Bridgetown Cricket Ground

Bridgetown, Somerset, England

Flanked by the River Exe and Exmoor National Park, and set in a dale hemmed round by hills, this beautiful ground is not short of recognition. In 1991 Jonathan Rice included it, or at least its pavilion, in his *Pavilion Book of Pavilions*; in 2002 it won *Wisden*'s Loveliest Cricket Ground award and in 2008 it received the *Daily Telegraph*'s Willow Walks Award for Best Village Ground. In July 2013 Liz Barrett from the BBC's Countryfile programme described it as, 'Quintessentially English, with spectacular views over Exmoor National Park and accessible by a wooden footbridge over the River Exe… even comes complete with its very own thatched-roof pavilion. Is this the perfect English cricket green?'

If you asked the club which award made it proudest, it probably wouldn't be any of those honours, but almost certainly winning the West Somerset League in 2014, its first title in 90 years of trying. By all accounts it was a close-run thing, won on countbacks 'after the most exciting finish ever,' according to the *Western Daily Press*.

Obviously, someone has been taking very good care of the ground over the years, and this turns out to be the club members themselves. Currently club secretary Doug Sherring and Kenny Cross do the bulk of the routine ground maintenance, though they didn't think their skills were up to replacing the old roof with a new one costing £6,000 in 2016.

Sherring, who has been with the club for several decades ('my only club'), remembers a very young Vic Marks playing a few games for the side. As well as its league commitments, the club hosts touring sides from as far away as Australia and Canada. Relations with the Everard Estate, which owns the ground, are very amicable and Guy Thomas-Everard is one of the club's vice-presidents.

The ground is accessible from the A396 by a narrow footbridge over a thin thread of the River Exe. Then it's a short walk to the pavilion with its thatched roof, oak panelling and rudimentary scoreboard and other facilities. Glancing back at Jonathan Rice's 1991 report, there is good news and bad news. The swallows and wrens, which he mentioned, still nest in the pavilion, which is good news, though they may not be the same ones. The not-so-good news is that the sanitary facilities are almost exactly the same. The dunny round the back, which Rice described as 'no bigger than a Buckingham Palace sentry box, but far less comfortable', has since been joined by a Ladies Portaloo. There are no showers either but, as Doug Sherring says, you can always jump in the Exe, and some team members do exactly that after a game.

Home to: Bridgetown Cricket Club

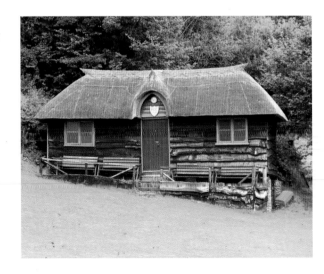

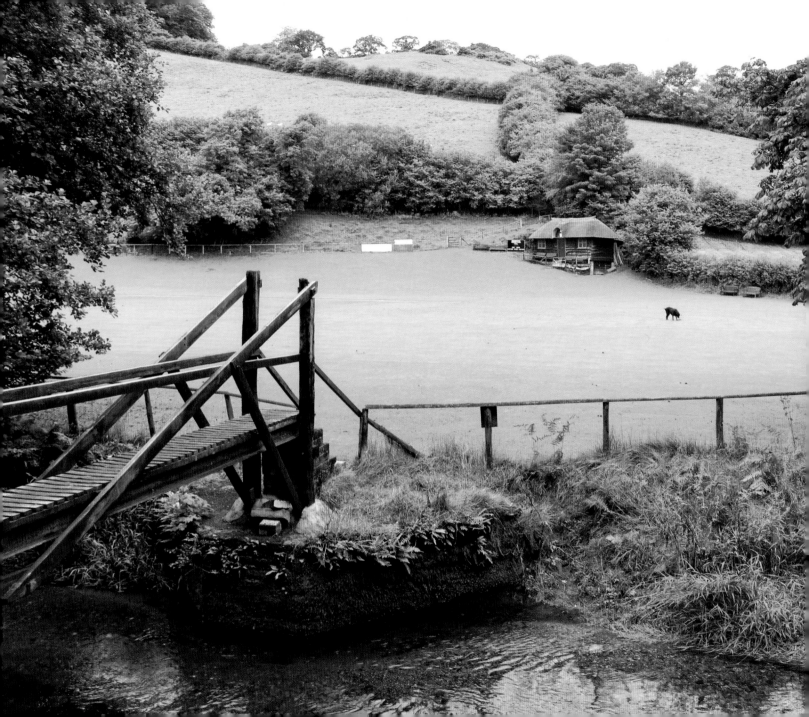

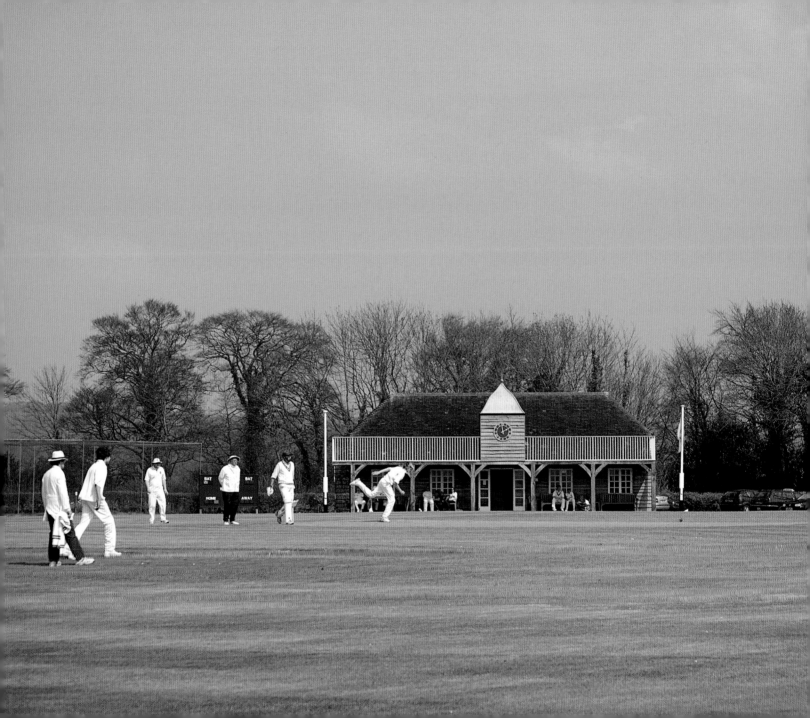

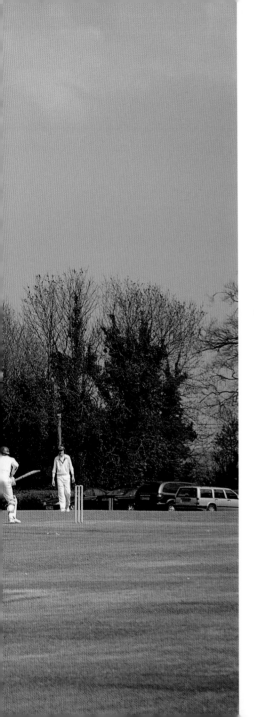

Broadhalfpenny Down

Hambledon, Hampshire, England

Hambledon Cricket Club, founded around 1750, has been described as 'the cradle of cricket'. In reality, other clubs were formed earlier but Hambledon became the most notable one in the late 18th century. The club had wealthy Hampshire patrons, and the Bat and Ball Inn was a legendary post-match retreat. The punch and ale were so strong that Richard Nyren, the landowner and publican, once said, 'It would put the souls of 10 tinkers into the body of a tailor.'

In the club's early days a cricket bat was curved like a banana and the wickets consisted of two stumps rather than three. The scorers cut notches in a stick to tally the runs, and the bowlers brought the ball up to their eye before delivering it underarm. When a Hambledon man made a good hit spectators shouted, in Hampshire accents, 'Go hard! Tich and turn!' In those days a lot of the game centred on betting, and even the local Hambledon vicar was known to have a flutter.

During the 1770s Hambledon had the best team in the country. Legend suggests that in 1775 Hambledon made so many runs that an All-England team gave up in despair. Two years later, a much stronger All-England team (146 and 187) beat Hambledon (117 and 162) by 54 runs. In 1778 Hambledon beat England by three wickets.

Until 1781 Hambledon played at Broadhalfpenny Down, between Winchester and Portsmouth. The venue's name is a corruption of 'bord-halfpenny', a type of fee paid in Anglo-Saxon times. In 1782 the club moved to Windmill Downs because Broadhalfpenny Down was 'too remote' from the village, a surprise in one sense as Broadhalfpenny had a pub opposite the ground but Windmill Down did not. The club had established and refined the laws of cricket, including the introduction of a third stump, but that role ended when the Marylebone Cricket Club (MCC) took over the sport's governance.

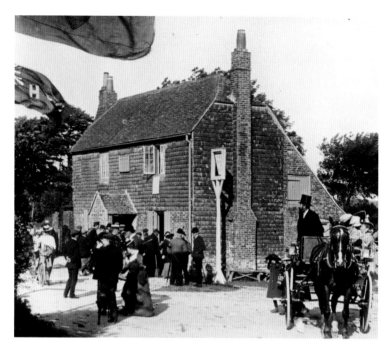

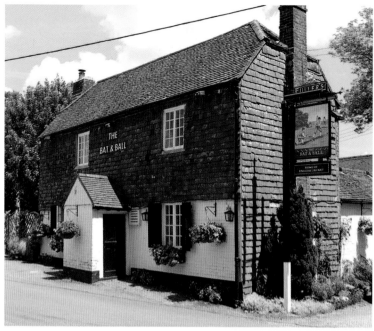

According to David Underdown, in his book *Start of Play*, Hambledon's decline in the late 18th century was caused by the impact of war with France, the migration of aristocratic patrons from Hampshire to London, and hardship in agriculture. Richard Nyren left Hambledon for a time in 1791 but was still living there in 1796, the year before his death. The club's final meeting was in 1797, when the wistful last minute read 'No gentlemen were present.'

Broadhalfpenny Down was used occasionally in the early half of the 20th century. In 1908 a match between Hambledon and an All-England XI took place, and a grey granite obelisk was unveiled by Mr E.M. Sprot (in the absence of W.G. Grace) to honour the club's past achievements. The stone's inscription reads:

THIS STONE MARKS THE SITE OF THE GROUND OF HAMBLEDON CRICKET CLUB CIRC. 1750–1787.

The old Hambledon ground was also the venue for a number of other one-off matches. Winchester College took over the land in July 1925 and that year a college side wore top hats for a match against Hambledon. On New Year's Day 1929 a match between Invalids and Hampshire Eskimos used a matting wicket while the hounds of a local hunt ran nearby

Two years later HMS *Nelson* played against Hambledon at Broadhalfpenny Down. The Navy team wore pig-tails, hard hats, check shirts and striped trousers, and Hambledon players wore top hats, knee breeches and buckled shoes.

After World War II the Royal Naval Signal School at HMS *Mercury* took over the lease of Broadhalfpenny Down, and, in 1958, some of the school's officers founded Broadhalfpenny Brigands Cricket Club. Since then the Brigands have used the cricket ground with the aim of promoting 'the continuation of cricket, played in a gentlemanly, sportsmanlike and friendly spirit on the historic ground at Broadhalfpenny Down'.

In 1992, the Hambledon Cricket Club records (minutes, subscription and account books for 1772 to 1796) went to the Hampshire County Record Office for safekeeping.

Home to: Broadhalfpenny Brigands Cricket Club

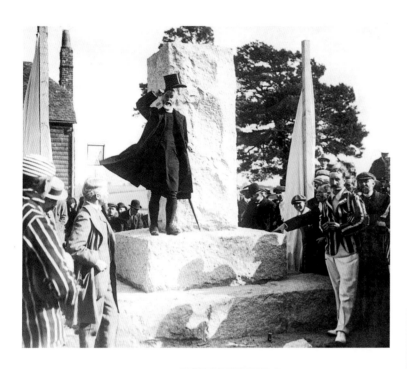

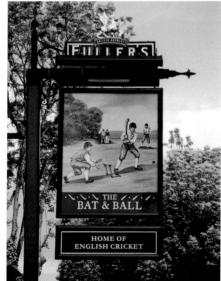

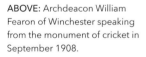

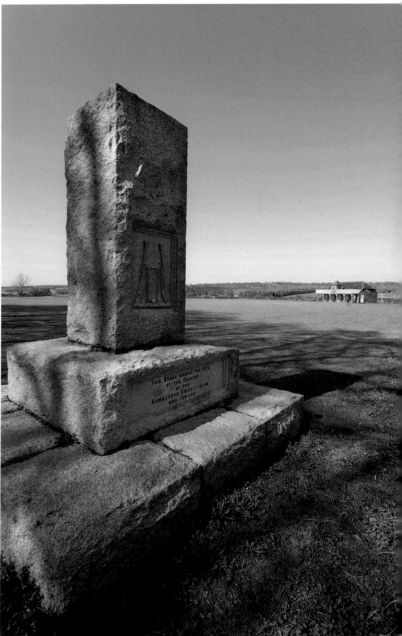

ABOVE: Archdeacon William Fearon of Winchester speaking from the monument of cricket in September 1908.

ABOVE LEFT: Hambledon's 18th-century Bat and Ball Inn, then (in 1908) and now.

FAR RIGHT: The monument marking the establishment of the Hambledon Cricket Club in 1750.

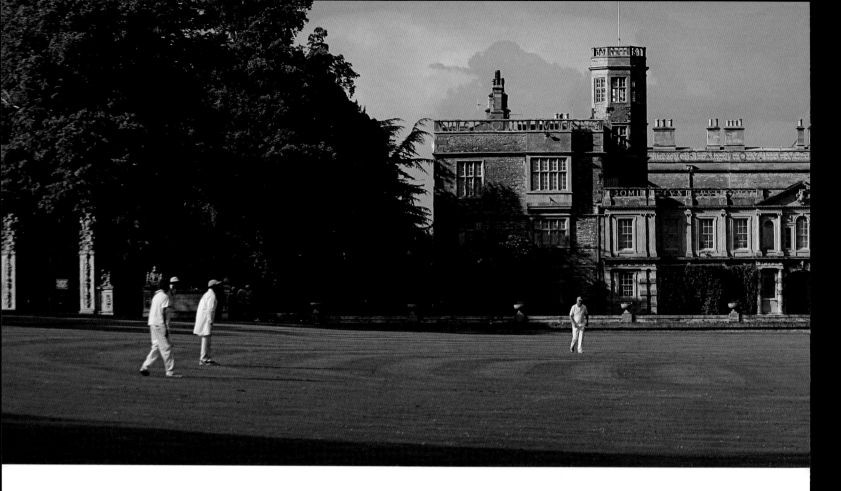

Castle Ashby House

Northamptonshire, England

Cricket was first played against the backdrop of this lovely building at the end of the 19th century when the staff of the house took on the stables and estate workers. Echoes of those games remain today in the annual game between a House and Gardens XI.

The building, once a manor house, began to grow in importance in the 14th century. Elizabeth I stayed there in 1600, and her successor, James I, in 1605. Its castellations entitle it to the formal name 'castle', but in truth it is more like an embellished mansion. Since the mid-16th century, the castle has belonged to the family of the Marquess of Northampton, whose family name is Compton, a famous cricketing name but no relation.

The original pavilion, built in 1904, was itself an architectural gem and discreetly positioned so that the then Earl couldn't see

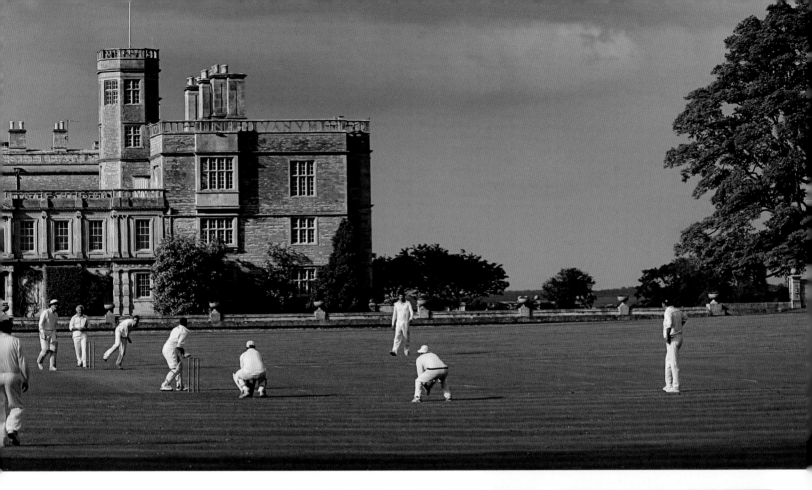

it from his bedroom. A more conveniently placed but less architecturally splendid pavilion was built in 1974, and paid for by a subscription donated by the sixth Marquess of Northampton. Relations between the team and the owners are as cordial as could be and don't require legalities such as a lease.

The playing area includes an ash tree which earns a six but only if hit on the full. The pitch, perhaps unusually, is end-on to the house, which is irreverently known as 'the shed end'. The boundary used to be a road running around the edge of a large field. These days the club takes mercy on its older players with a few strategically placed markers to cut off the corners, much appreciated if there has been some conviviality in the village the night before. The club has a cheerful quirky element. With two home-bred Mark Hendersons in the side, in 2021 it's planned to field a full team of Mark Hendersons - at the time of writing they're already up to 8. Fun for everyone except the scorer!

Home to: Castle Ashby Cricket Club

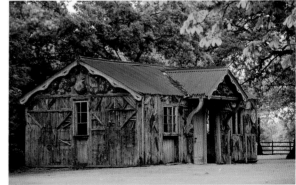

Chail Cricket Ground

Himachal Pradesh, India

In terms of cricketing activity, Chail cricket ground boasts more of a past than a present.

The ground's genesis was certainly different. In or about 1891, the story goes that Lord Kitchener and the Maharajah of Patiala, Bhupinder Singh, had a row. Since Kitchener was serving in Egypt at that time and did not arrive in India till 1902, possibly the grandee concerned was the 5th Marquess of Lansdowne, the then Viceroy.

The Marquess had a short way with those who crossed him and in 1890 executed the leader of a local insurrection. He punished the Maharajah by denying him access to the summer capital, Shimla. The Maharajah fled to nearby Chail, where he built a new summer retreat for himself, including cricket facilities for matches against the British. At 2,286 metres (7,500 feet), it was the highest ground in the world.

Prior to World War II, a later Maharajah passed the buildings back to the government and they became army property and ultimately Rashtriya Military School. Ironically, this

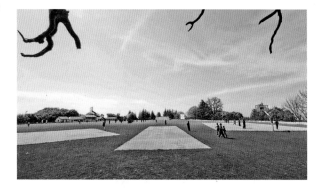

particular Maharajah, also called Bhupinder Singh, had a very good cricketing pedigree and captained India on its 1911 tour of England. Today the military presence is still very much in evidence with barracks around the boundary and a helipad where deep mid-off was once positioned. Unsurprisingly, entrance is forbidden. Some cricket is still played by cadets and children for which there is an extensive sight screen and large scoreboard. The field also doubles up as a polo ground. Chail's claim to be the highest ground in the world is not recognised by the Guinness Book of Records due to the absence of regular competitive cricket.

The historic tree in the grounds, like those in Canterbury and Pietermaritzburg, used to lie within the boundary. Though now deceased and encased in concrete, it was once a glorious Banj oak, an evergreen oak from the western slopes of the central Himalaya, often found with rhododendrons, pines and walnuts.

Home to: Rashtriya Military School

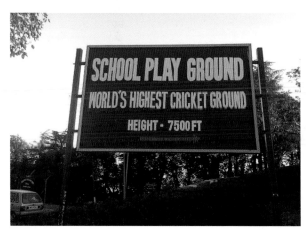

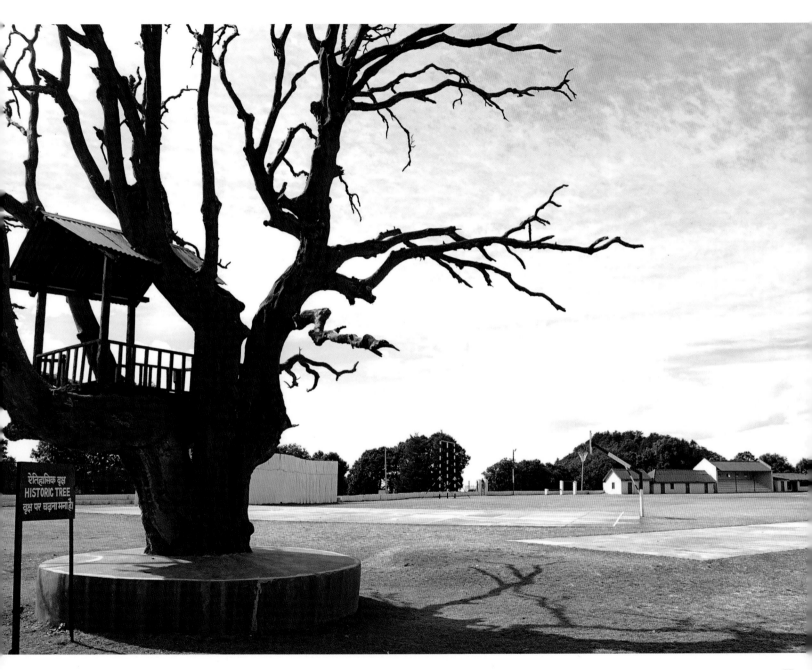

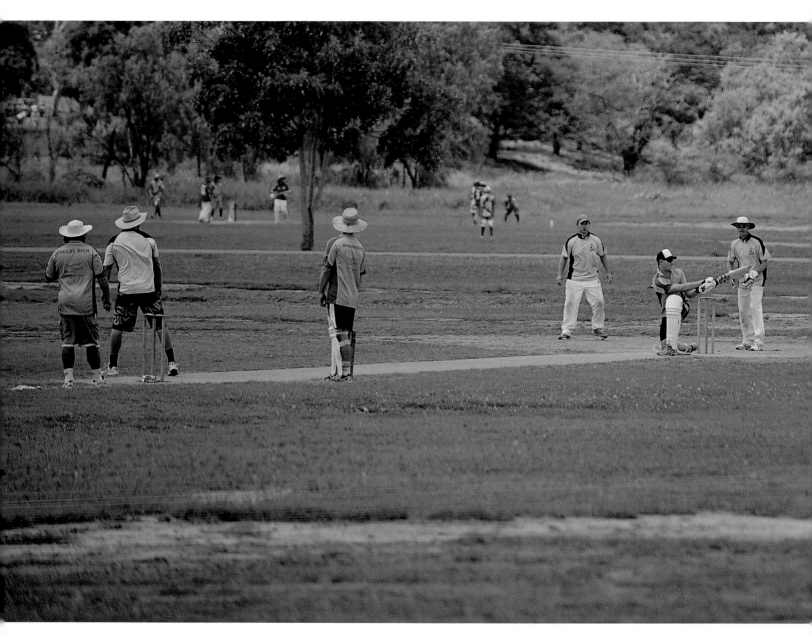

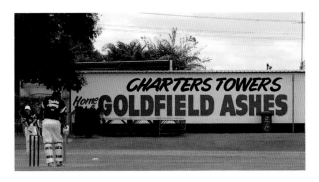

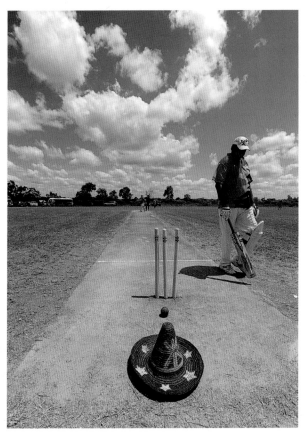

Charters Towers Goldfield Ashes

Queensland, Australia

Towards the end of the 19th century, the city of Charters Towers was the centre of Australia's richest gold field with a population of over 30,000 people. The boom petered out long ago and today the figure is nearer 10,000.

But on a long weekend towards the end of each January, that number is augmented by several thousand when cricket teams from all over the country come to the town to compete in the Goldfield Ashes, the largest competition of its type in the southern hemisphere.

First held in 1949, over 200 sides now take part. Team names include A Fish Called Wanda, Seriously Pist, Bigger than Jesus, Benaud's Boys, Unbeerlievable and, from the women's section, More Ass than Class, which seems accurate as in 2016 the side came bottom of its league. Each team plays three matches and complicated rules are in place to engineer a result even when rain is about. The A Grade, which plays a Twenty20 format, is very competitive, as are some of the other leagues, which play 50-over matches. But some sides are more laid back. Not all have the full range of equipment, like pads, and some male players get more out of the occasion playing in dresses. Even though the organisers issue stern requests with lots of words in bold capitals for the participants NOT to take alcohol on to the field, ESPECIALLY if umpiring, in the lower leagues some have been seen playing with a beer in one hand.

With over 70 grounds in play, from the main ground to schools and private properties, the playing conditions can be variable but it's a good few days and Charters Towers welcomes the return of the boom times, if only for the weekend.

Home to: The Charters Towers Goldfield Ashes

City Oval

Pietermaritzburg, South Africa

A visit to the City Oval in Alexandra Park is like stepping back in time to the height of Victorian splendour. The eye is immediately caught by the splendid twin-turreted pavilion built in 1898 to commemorate the 60th anniversary of the founding of the city. The adjacent bandstand adds to the illusion and it is easy to imagine it in the days when moustachioed wind players performed selections from Gilbert and Sullivan. Established in 1863 to mark the engagement of the future Edward VII to Princess Alexandra of Denmark, after whom the park is named, the ground is designated a national monument. William Lucas, its designer, used the Queen's Park cricket ground in Chesterfield as a model.

Able to hold 12,000 spectators, it is surprising that it has never hosted a Test match and only two ODIs, in the 2003 World Cup, although much first-class cricket is played on the ground.

The City Oval is one of only three first-class grounds to have had a tree within its boundary, the other two being St Lawrence Cricket Ground, Canterbury, England and the VRA Ground, Amstelveen, the Netherlands. Uniquely, however, the ground invites any cricketer who scores a century or takes five wickets in an innings to plant a tree, though outside the boundary.

On leaving the ground, there is still over 200 acres of Alexandra Park to explore with its wide variety of plants, such as jacarandas and azaleas.

Home to: KwaZulu-Natal Inland, KwaZulu-Natal and the Dolphins

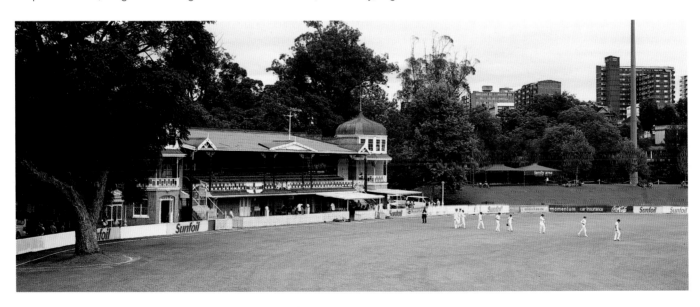

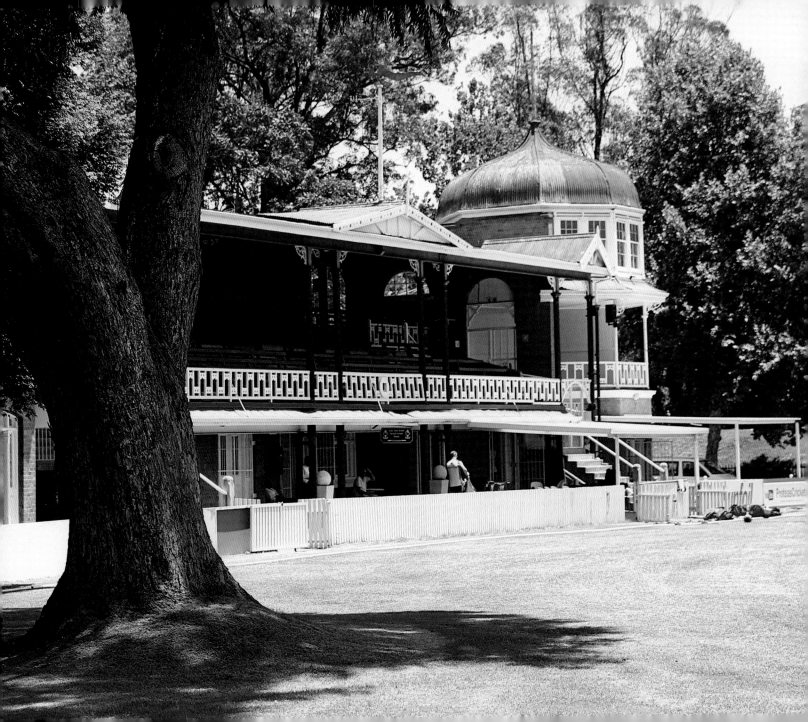

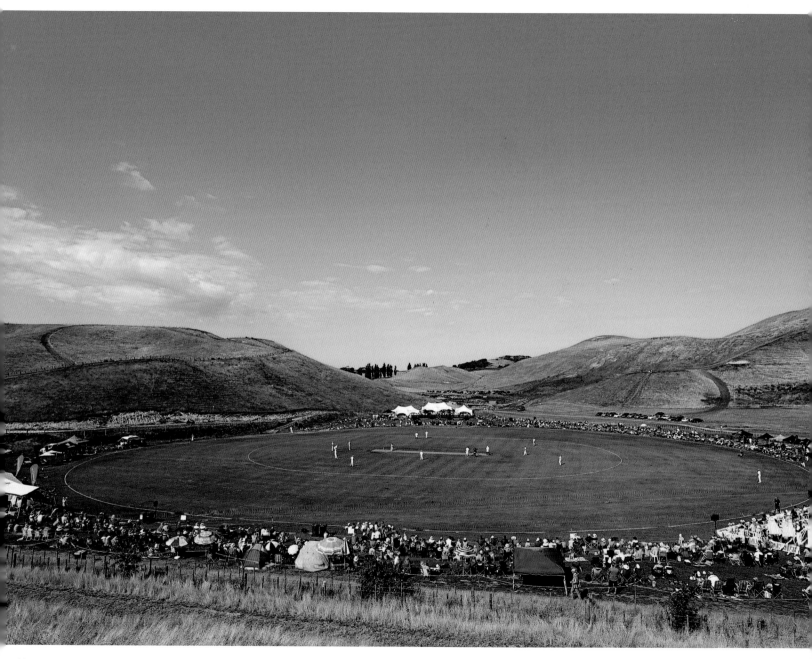

Clifton County Cricket Club

Te Awanga, North Island, New Zealand

The CCCC ground has a relatively short history – cricket has only been played here since 1985 – but in that time it has won many admirers. Suresh Menon, editor of *Wisden India*, reportedly rated it as the most beautiful he had visited anywhere in the world, and professional cricket writers like Menon are certainly spoiled for choice.

The ground was the brainchild of a local farmer and a friend. They gazed out at the natural amphitheatre encircled by idyllic rolling hills. Within easy walking distance was a spectacular view of the South Pacific. Wonderful wines were produced in the area. They thought how wonderful it would be to create a ground in such surroundings for themselves and their friends.

With a lot of hard work, determination and local support this was achieved. But it was the next generation of the founders who took things a stage further. A much-needed ground irrigation system was introduced, to counter the arid summer conditions, and an all-weather pitch laid. Urban youngsters were offered coaching so they would get out into the countryside and were also taught about the need for conservation. Though cricket is always primary, the organisers are involved in several projects, including the planting of 15,000 trees as part of a significant biodiversity programme.

The current managers insist the club is about a lot more than cricket. According to club secretary Sam Howard, it's a three-pronged project about conservation, recreation and agriculture.

Clifton is now a recognised port-of-call for cricket lovers and a constant stream of visitors come to see and admire. The ground was selected to host one of the side matches to the 2015 Cricket World Cup, the local team playing a celebrity side consisting of former Test players, All Blacks, and TV personalities, captained by Australian fast bowler Jeff Thomson. The game was called the Cricket Art Deco Match because Napier, a nearby town, is an Art Deco marvel. Players and spectators joined in the fun, dressing up in period clothes.

Home to: Clifton County Cricket Club

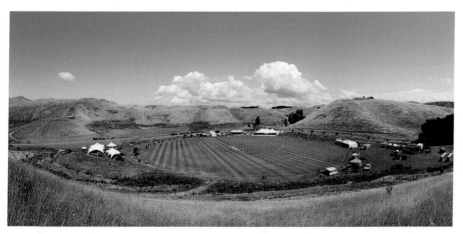

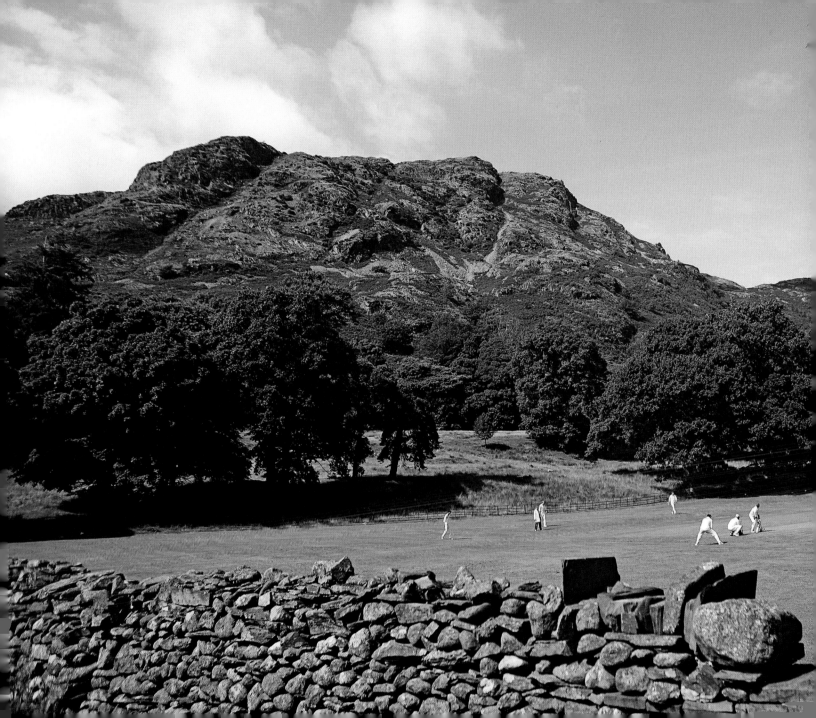

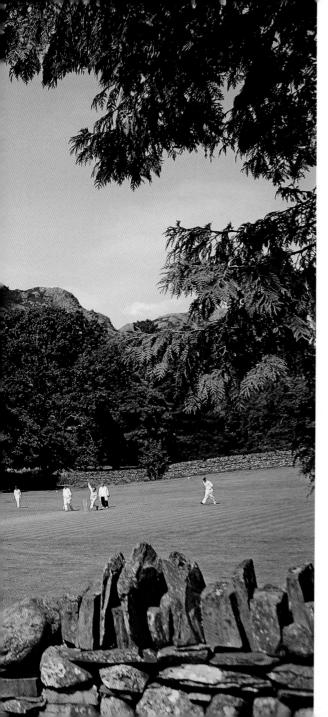

Coniston Cricket Ground

Coniston, Cumbria, England

Set in the Lake District National Park, Coniston cricket ground is dominated by a stunning view of Yewdale Crag. The locale is full of impressive features such as the the Old Man of Coniston, which rises dramatically behind the houses and dominates the village. It is a favourite area for walkers and climbers and has attracted tourists since the introduction of the railways in the Victorian era.

The area has associations with many famous people. John Ruskin (1819-1900), the art critic, philanthropist and social thinker, lived locally and is buried in Coniston. Beatrix Potter (1866-1943), the writer best known for her children's books, owned an estate nearby and Donald Campbell (1921-67), the speed record breaker, was killed on nearby Coniston Water trying to break his own water speed record. *Swallows and Amazons*, the famous children's book by Arthur Ransome, is based on locations in the area and indeed the irascible Ransome learned to sail on Coniston.

If Coniston cricket ground is dominated by Yewdale Crag, off the field the dominating topic of conversation for too long had been the need for a new pavilion. The club had been desperate for some time to replace its small, ageing pavilion with something more suitable for its ambitions. Founded in 1890, the club plays in Divisions 2 and 4 of the Westmorland Cricket League and have had their share of successes over the years. It now runs three sides - first and second

teams and junior boys, which desperately needed better and more modern facilities. With the involvement of Grizedale Arts and helped by Olympic Legacy funding, a competition for a replacement was launched which attracted over 80 entries. The original plan was for a timber-clad building with a cricket bat theme, but this was amended through the planning process to a more conventional pavilion costing around £40,000. Money was raised through grants and local fundraising and much of the work was carried out by electricians, plumbers, joiners and painters from the club. The new pavilion was opened in time for the 2019 season and also acts as a community resource where schoolchildren can come for art classes in one of the most beautiful landscapes in the country.

Former chairman Nigel Dixon acts as groundsman with plenty of help from volunteers. Nigel says the club has a lot of time for David Lloyd, the TV broadcaster and former England coach and Test player, and well remembers the long journey Lloyd made from Plymouth to attend a function, all without asking for a fee.

The club suffered a sad loss in late 2019, when Nathan Atkinson - very heavily involved in all the club's activities as captain, secretary and treasurer - died in a farming accident at the age of 26, a devastating blow for the club.

Home to: Coniston Cricket Club

Crooklets Cricket Ground

Bude, Cornwall, England

Cricket has been played in this beautiful clifftop setting overlooking the Atlantic since at least 1859. Originally called Bude-Stratton CC, the club dates back to 1870, but changed its name to North Cornwall CC in 1958 and later to Bude North Cornwall. Stratton shrugs at its lack of recognition and responds with a local saying, 'Stratton was a market town when Bude was just a furzy down.'

With strong south-westerlies to contend with, it is no easy matter to organise cricket. Starting in January, club chairman Tony Greaves and the club's groundstaff volunteers spend 35 to 40 hours a week preparing the ground. They admit that the wicket is a bit of a batting paradise. 'You should be able to get 250 in a 50-overs game,' says Greaves.

The wind can be a real problem and one bowler ended up by bowling 18 wides in an over. Bowl from the Crooklets Beach end, is the local advice. On one occasion the covers were on overnight and next morning they had disappeared only to turn up in the public car park. On field communication means fielders sometimes have to resort to tic-tac. But the wind also means the ground is very fast-drying. Surface water disappears within an hour.

Since 2014, the club has a new pavilion to be proud of, opened by Phil Vickery, the former England rugby captain who comes from Bude. The first pavilion, erected in 1883, was replaced in the 1930s. When its successor

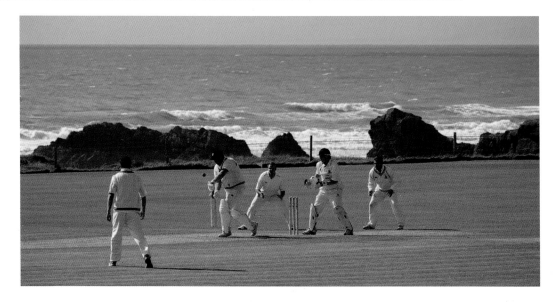

started showing its age, the council financed the building of a new one, helped by grant funding from Sport England, which has also helped provide finance for pitches, coaching equipment, covers and sightscreens. The results are certainly visible on the pitch, as the 2015 season was one of the club's best.

The beauty of the location is known all over the world and requests to play friendlies come in all the time. Some are declined, but one visitor who was always welcome was the late Brian Johnston who used to holiday in Bude and attended the matches.

Greaves can hardly believe his luck. 'It is spectacular to play here. And the pavilion

is state of the art!' The boundary line is just inside the wire fence. On the other side of the fence, plenty of walkers enjoy a stroll along the cliff top between Crooklets Beach and Summerleaze Beach. With the Atlantic only 30 metres (100 feet) away, they may wonder if a six carried by the wind has ever made it into the waves. 'Not yet,' says Greaves, 'but with the new massive bats, it'll happen sooner or later.'

In 2020 Somerset CCC organised a competition to find the Best Club Ground in the south-west and Bude edged out Sidmouth and Dorchester for the crown.

Home to: Bude North Cornwall Cricket Club

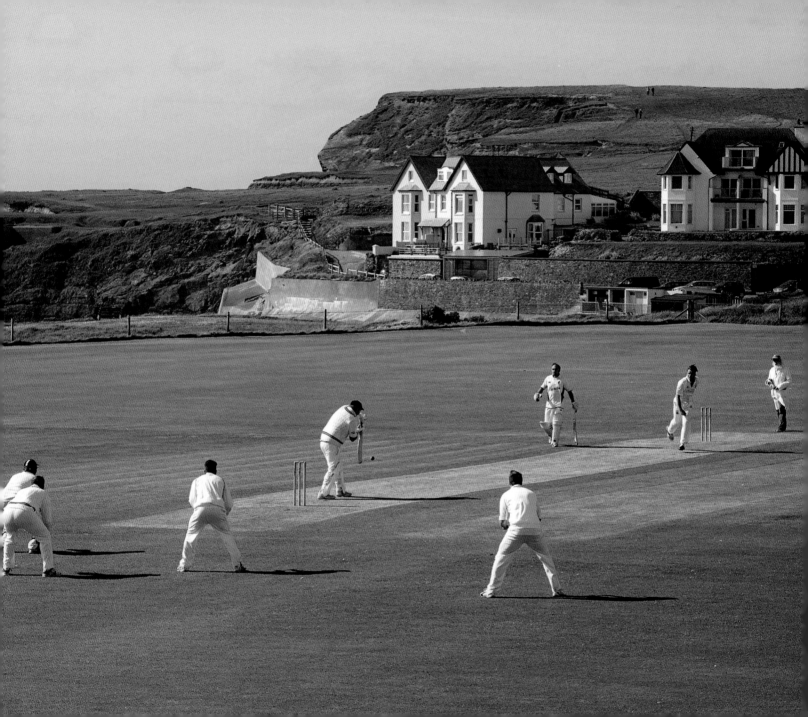

Darren Sammy National Cricket Ground

Saint Lucia, West Indies

Formerly the Beausejour Stadium, the ground was renamed the Darren Sammy National Cricket Ground in honour of the Saint Lucian captain of the West Indies team which won the World Twenty20 in 2016. One of the stands has been named after another Saint Lucian member of the side, Johnson Charles, who also received a plot of land.

The Windward Islands are not a great power, even in Caribbean cricket, but their stadium has been highly praised for its features and facilities. Funded by cash from the island's lottery, it is a splendid resource for an island of 184,000 people. Opened in 2002 and designed locally, the stadium, sited in the shadow of the Beausejour Hills, can hold 20,000 spectators. Some of its features are very much top-of-the-range with the pavilion having a lounge, balcony, conference room and gym for both sides. The outfield is described as 'a perfectly lush-green oval'. Brian Lara said the ground was possibly the best in the Caribbean. Saint Lucian artist Sir Dunstan St. Omer, designer of the country's national flag and creator of epic murals, was awed by 'the majesty, the grandeur, the beauty of the stadium'. 'Though I am not a cricketer,' he observed, 'seeing the stadium was a defining moment, a celebration of the hopes and aspirations of the people of Saint Lucia.'

Within a year of its opening, the stadium was hosting the first of four Tests to have been played here. Brian Lara found the ground very much to his liking, scoring 209 against Sri Lanka in a drawn game. The ground was England's base in the 2007 World Cup and hosted seven games in all, including a semi-final. In 2006, it was the first venue in the Caribbean to host a day-night game.

Test matches have brought great players like Sangakkara, Sehwag, Muralitharan, Dravid and Dhoni to the island. Big names have played for the St Lucia Zouks in the Caribbean Premier League Twenty20 competition. Kevin Pietersen signed up for 2015 and the squad for 2016 included Shane Watson, Morne Morkel, Fidel Edwards and local hero and sole Test player, Darren Sammy.

It would be nice to know what a Zouk is, though.

Home to: Windward Islands, St Lucia Zouks

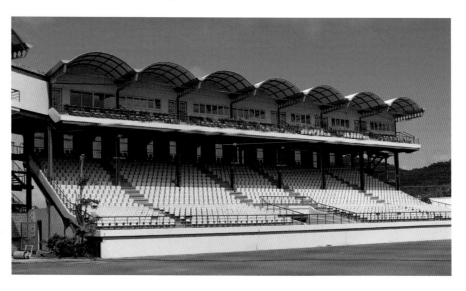

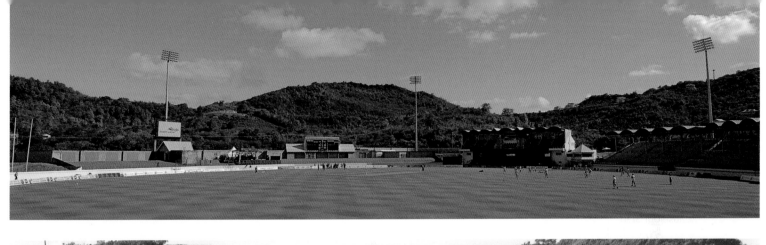

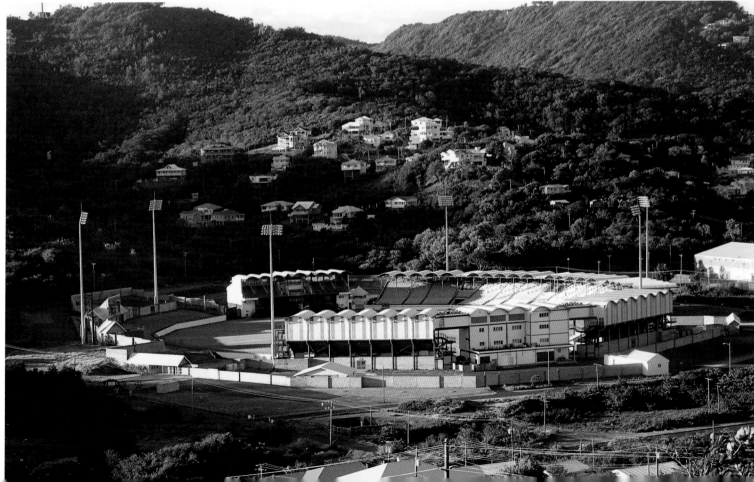

Eden Gardens

Kolkata, India

Eden Gardens stands in more than 50 acres of blissful landscape, including small arched bridges, avenues of slender palm trees and a Burmese pagoda. But until the British cleared it in the mid-18th century, the area was a jungle.

The enormous cricket ground was once the second largest in the world after Melbourne, but redevelopment in 2009 reduced its capacity from about 100,000 to 66,000, though now it is up to 68,000. Home to the most passionate and vocal crowd in the game, it still seems to retain a unique febrile quality. On good days, the spectators' energy acts like a 12th man for the Indian cricket team. On bad, the supporters can turn militant, earning the ground a raucous reputation.

Designed in 1841, Eden Gardens is named after the Eden sisters, Fanny and Emily. The latter wrote extensively about her travels in India. They were sisters of Lord Auckland, the Governor-General of India between 1836 and 1842. The ground itself was established in 1864 and has been called India's 'answer to the Coliseum'. It has hosted more Tests than any other Indian ground, and faced at least two major crises in recent years, one cricketing and the other organisational.

The cricketing crisis took place in a Test against Pakistan in 1999, when Sachin Tendulkar was run out after colliding with the blindingly fast Shoaib Akhtar as he tried to complete a third run. According to Martin Williamson writing for ESPN Cricinfo, 'the neutral's view seemed to be that it was a genuine accident'. The crowd in Eden Park weren't neutral, of course, and after the game turned decisively in Pakistan's favour, 'spectators started burning newspapers in the stands and hurled fruit and plastic bottles onto the field' according to *Wisden*, and the ground had to be cleared. The following day Pakistan completed its victory in front of about 200 people. Even prior to this unfortunate incident, riots had disrupted matches on at least two occasions.

The organisational crisis related to improving the ground to meet the ICC's standards for the 2011 World Cup. Plans included a new clubhouse and players' facilities, upgrading the exterior walls to give the stadium a new look, and re-cladding the existing roof structure. The first game was to be India v. England on 27 February, but on 25 January the *Times of India* painted a picture of Eden Gardens 'in shambles… with heavy iron beams, bricks and mortar and tons of rubbish lying all over the stadium … less than 24 hours before the ICC delegation's visit'. Add the work still to be done to the Press Box, VIP enclosures, toilets and other facilities, and the situation did not look good. Unsurprisingly, the ground officials are reported to have said there was nothing to worry about. In the event, the ground suffered the humiliation of the ICC transferring the first game from Eden Park to Bengaluru. The subsequent three matches in March were able to take place as planned, although the third match, Kenya v. Zimbabwe, had the lowest recorded tickets purchased in the stadium's history with only 15 spectators buying tickets.

With all its ups and downs, Eden Park has been the scene of some famous cricketing occasions. A remarkable innings occurred in November 2014 on the 150th anniversary of the ground when Rohit Sharma scored 264 off 173 balls in an ODI against Sri Lanka. The ground also staged an emotional farewell to Sachin Tendulkar on his 199th and penultimate Test appearance in November 2013, welcoming him with 199 roses. It hosted the first ever day-night Test in India in 2019.

Home to: Bengal Cricket Team

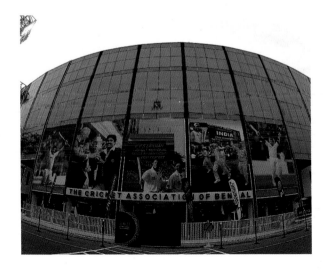

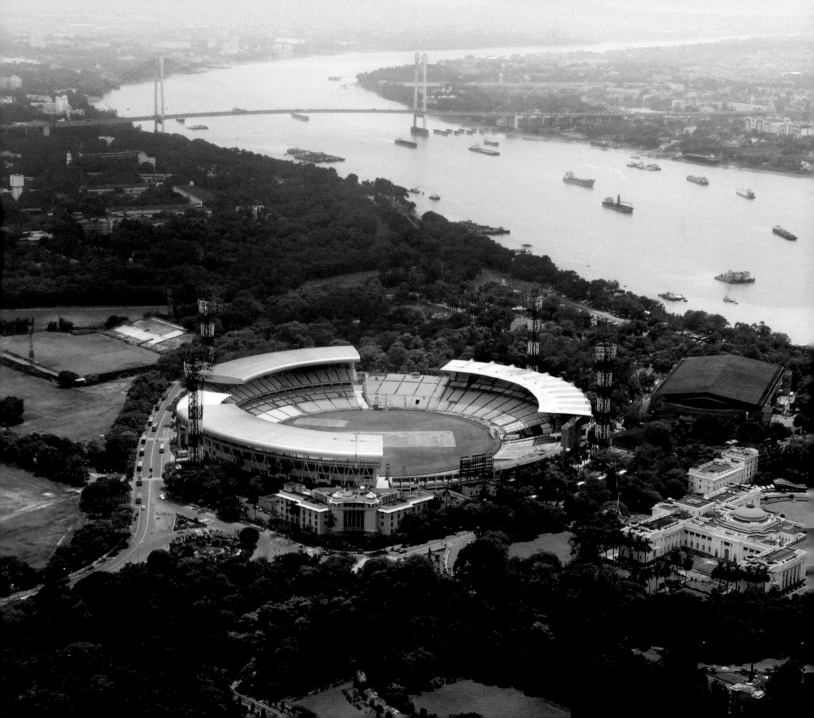

Emerald Headingley Stadium

Leeds, Yorkshire, England

Some remarkable Test matches have taken place at Headingley. Bradman twice scored a triple century here; once in 1930 in his fifth game for Australia – the only time a Test batsman has scored 300 runs in a single day – and once in 1934 when he scored 304. Dear to the heart of older supporters, especially Yorkshiremen, is the memory of Freddie Trueman reducing India to nought for four in the second innings of the first Test in 1952. In 1977, Geoffrey Boycott brought the ground to its feet when he scored his hundredth first-class hundred during the fourth Test against Australia. In 1991 Graham Gooch scored a brilliant 154 not out against the West Indies, enabling England to beat the West Indies at home for the first time in 22 years. Perhaps the most thrilling occasion of all was the Ashes test of 1981 when Botham and Willis defied odds of 500 to one to win a game that, by conventional measures, was basically a lost cause.

Headingley was founded in 1890 and hosted its first Test in 1899 against Australia. More than most Test grounds, it has a certain unpredictability and quirkiness. At Trent Bridge, Lord's and the Oval, if captains win the toss, they almost always bat first. At Headingley, if you win the toss you look up at the cloud cover and wonder. To the cricket lover, it has always been fun anticipating a Test at Headingley.

In recent years attention has been less on the cricket and more on whether the ground

has a future at all. In 2011 the club's financial situation was so dire that it announced that it would not bid for Tests for the 2013 and 2015 Ashes series. To the outsider it seemed bizarre that any club with the opportunity to bid for an Ashes Test would choose not to do so. But with the organisation seriously underfunded, the Chairman Colin Graves decided that he could not afford to put the club at risk.

Up to 2005, Yorkshire CCC didn't even own the ground at all. Then it paid £12 million to purchase the freehold, borrowing £9 million from Leeds County Council to finance it. The situation is complicated by local geography. On the southern side of the cricket ground is an adjoining stadium, also called Headingley, but home to two rugby teams – Leeds Rhinos from the rugby league code and Yorkshire Carnegie from rugby union. The South Stand

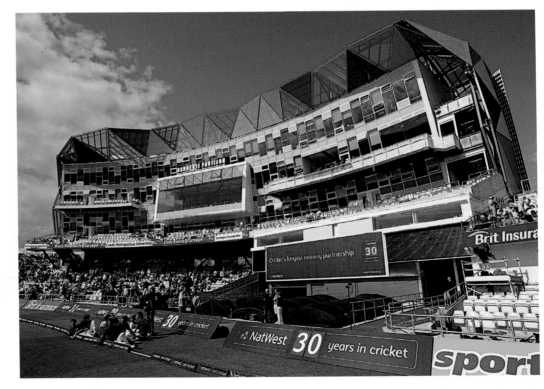

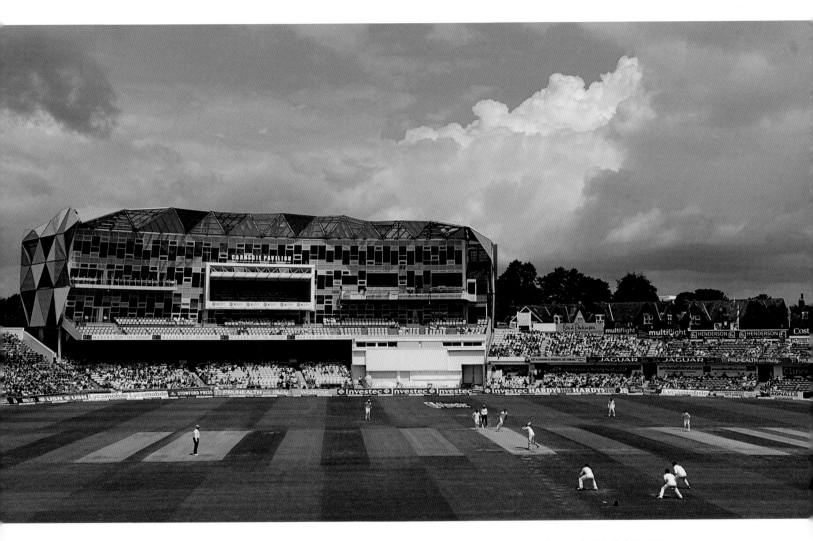

of the cricket ground is the North Stand of the rugby ground and it is often referred to as the North/South Stand. So the two sports share common features, not unlike Siamese twins. To make things worse, in 2015 this joint stand, some of it dating back to 1932, was discovered to have corrosion. Total closure for safety reasons was a possibility,

but, in the event, just a few rows in the cricket stand were roped off pending the rebuilding of the stand, which re-opened in May 2019. The new North/South Stand was the second phase of a six-phase redevelopment project and the grand plan may take as long as 20 years to complete and with an estimated cost of £50 million.

Already in place is the 2010 Carnegie Pavilion, multi-faceted like an extravagant gemstone. The design concept, according to the architects, is 'a soft, green cricket glove gripping a ball,' though not everybody agrees. The building has a dual use. The prime funders of the pavilion, Leeds Beckett University, specified that the space should be

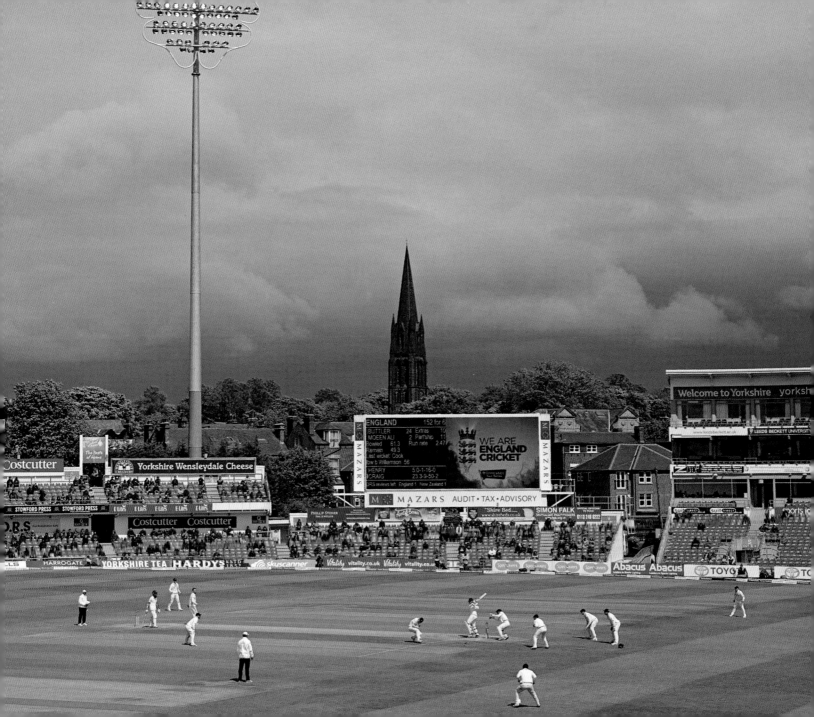

used as classrooms for some of its courses, so the building gets far more use than the average cricket facility.

Headingley began hosting Ashes series again in 2019 and was witness to one of the most extraordinary matches in Ashes history. England won by a single wicket. After scoring only 67 in their first innings, they scored 362/9 in the 2nd, with Ben Stokes 135 not out and Jack Leach on a stubborn 1 not out (from 17 balls) putting on an unbeaten stand of 76 to win the match. Headingley is scheduled to host Tests in the non-Ashes years of 2021 and 2022 and an Ashes Test in 2023.

Home to: Yorkshire County Cricket Club

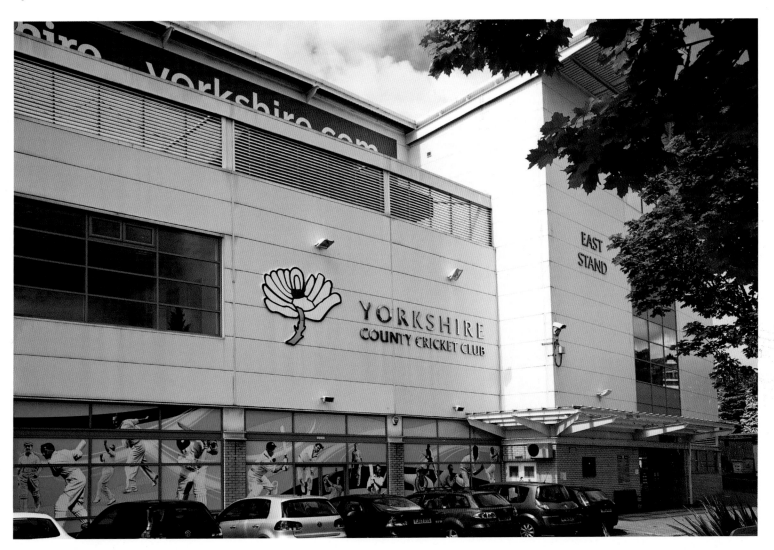

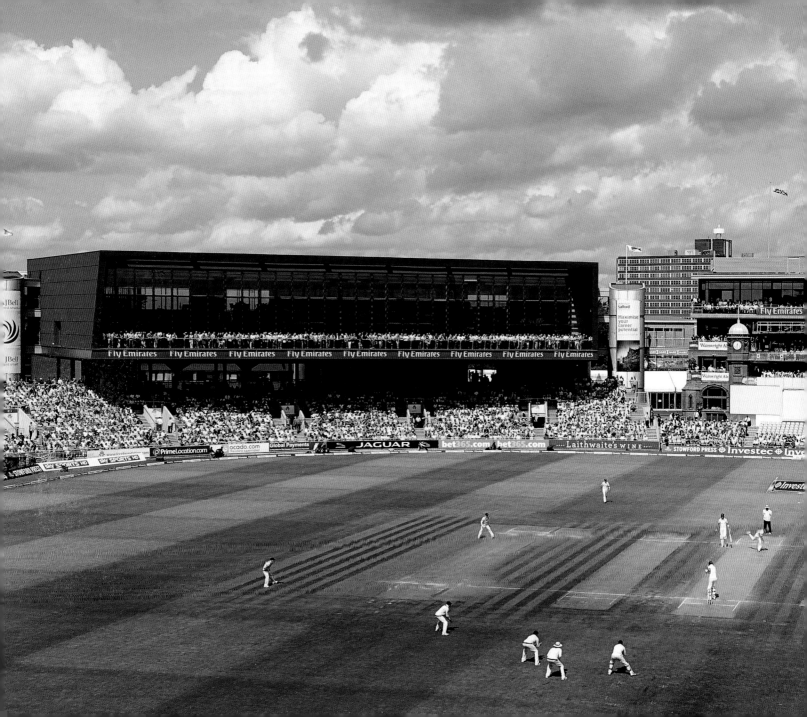

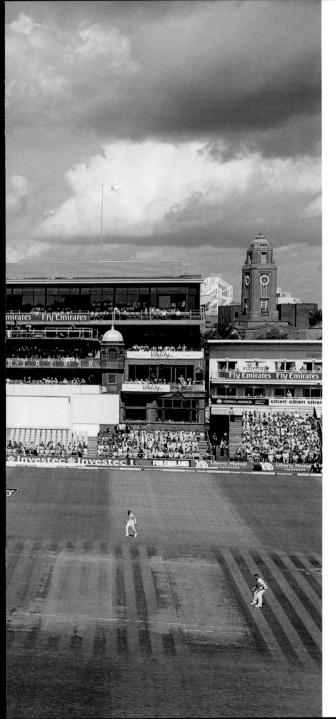

Emirates Old Trafford

Greater Manchester, England

Emirates Old Trafford, the home of Lancashire County Cricket Club, is one of the great Test-playing venues in the world. Cricket was first played here in 1857 by Manchester Cricket Club, the forerunner of Lancashire CCC. The ground is the third oldest Test venue in the world and, back in 1884, the first ever Ashes Test in England was held here. It is named after the de Trafford family who owned the ground until 1898.

Historic moments are plentiful. In 1956 Jim Laker strolled off the field, sweater slung carelessly over his shoulder, having taken 10 wickets in an innings and 19 wickets in an Ashes Test. In 1981 Ian Botham scored 118 in the Fifth Ashes Test, one of his greatest Test innings, and in 1990 the 17-year-old Sachin Tendulkar scored the first of his record 51 Test hundreds. Shane Warne, on his first tour of England in 1999, bowled Mike Gatting with his first ball in an Ashes Test, always remembered as the Ball of the Century.

But, despite Old Trafford's outstanding cricket pedigree, ground development fell behind. In the early 2000s, more modern venues, such as the Emirates Riverside, Durham; Sophia Gardens, Cardiff; and the Ageas Bowl, Southampton, were keen to hold Test matches and were investing huge

sums for that purpose. In 2008 Old Trafford was officially warned by the ECB that unless it substantially renewed itself, it would be dropped from the rota in favour of one of the newer grounds. Very likely this would have meant the end not only of Test cricket but of all cricket at Old Trafford.

When options of building a new stadium elsewhere fell through, the club realised that the only course was to redevelop the existing ground. This proposal ran up against legal opposition and at one stage the club took a gamble that a crucial permission would be granted in order to receive substantial development grants. The whole process required strong nerves and strong leadership provided by Jim Cumbes, the Chief Executive, who had played cricket for Lancashire and kept goal for Aston Villa.

Eventually the massive process of re-modernisation began. One of the features that most attracted attention was the early decision to rotate the pitch from an east-west axis to north-south, the final championship club to do so. At long last the pavilion, which had been lateral to the pitch, was now looking down the pitch and the long-suffering members could at least see if there was any ball movement.

Batsmen were pleased too, as the setting sun no longer dazzled them. The square has increased to accommodate 15 wickets. The redevelopment began in 2009 and is still in process but much has been achieved, including two new grandstands, two media centres, a redesigned pavilion, improved drainage, permanent floodlights and a new scoreboard. The design is futuristic, Cumbes says, and with a northern flavour. There is certainly no shortage of bold red symbolising the Lancashire red rose.

The ground is in the ECB's good books again and has hosted Ashes and other Tests. So all the problems seem to have been sorted, except perhaps for one. Facing prevailing winds and weather from the Atlantic, Old Trafford has reputedly one of the worst records for rain. Two Tests, in 1890 and 1938, were completely rained off (although they were not five-day games). The second occasion may be one of the earliest examples of a drop-in pitch as the ground staff desperately tried to replace the pitch on the main square with one from a practice pitch, albeit unsuccessfully.

The pavilion end was renamed the James Anderson end in 2018 in honour of England player James Anderson, the most successful fast bowler in Test history. Anderson went on to claim a historic 600th wicket, dismissing captain Azhar Ali in the third Test against Pakistan in August 2020.

Home to: Lancashire County Cricket Club

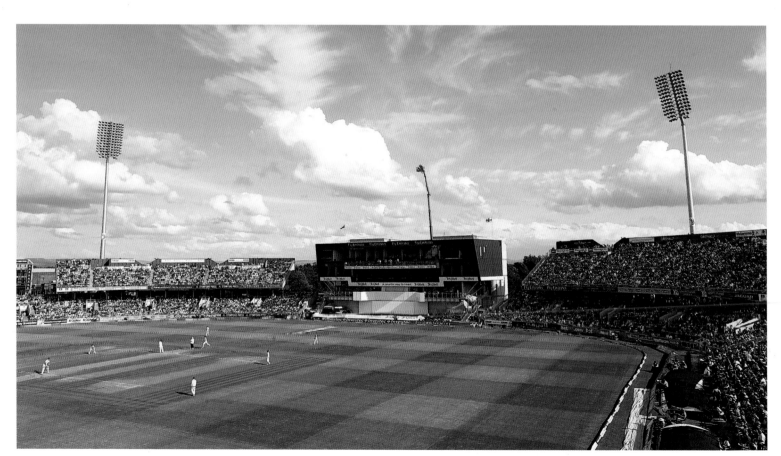

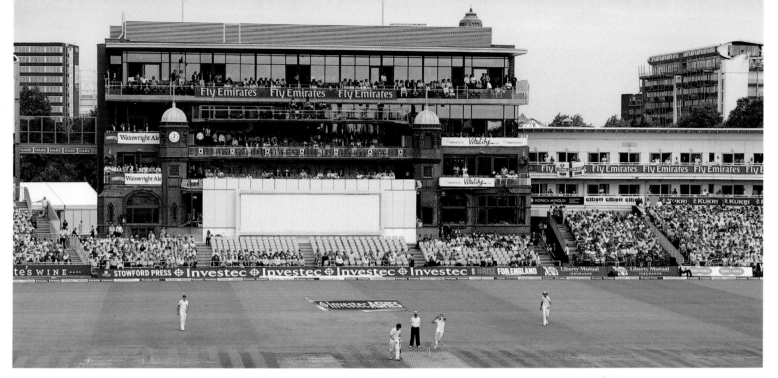

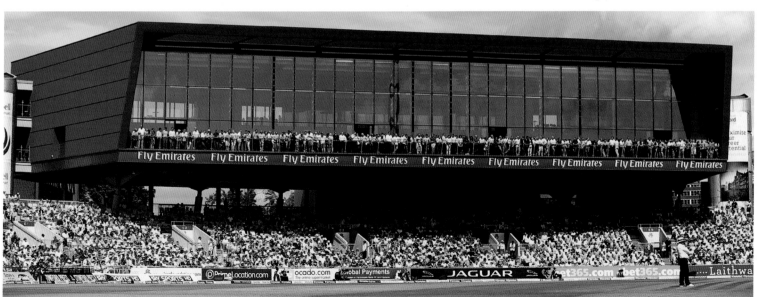

Feroz Shah Kotla Ground

Delhi, India

Feroz Shah Kotla ground, once known as the Willingdon Pavilion after a former Viceroy, is the second oldest stadium in India after Eden Gardens. Located near the centre of the city on the edge of Old Delhi, it is situated within the walled citadel of the fortress erected in 1356 by Sultan Feroz Shah Tughlaq after whom the ground is named. Fortified gates and barbican towers all around are reminders of the past. The fortress sits on the banks of the Yamuna River, which, 200 kilometres (125 miles) downstream, drifts past the Taj Mahal.

Used for cricket by the English from 1883, the ground hosted its first Test in 1948 against the West Indies, the first Test match in post-independence India. The home country is particularly successful here. It has won 10 out of the last 12 Tests and drawn the other two, while winning all seven of the most recent ODIs. England also found it very much to their liking in the 2016 World Twenty20 when they beat Sri Lanka, scraped past Afghanistan and then went on to beat New Zealand in the semi-final.

The ground, owned and managed by the DDCA (Delhi District Cricket Association), has had its controversies over the years, particularly in 2009 when an ODI between India and Sri Lanka was called off after a few overs because the pitch was deemed unfit to play on.

Its capacity of 41,820 puts it in the top 15 largest cricket stadiums in the world and it has a slightly idiosyncratic feel with the vast unmistakeable North Stand towering over the ground, bearing some resemblance to the cross-section of a multi-storey car park. It was constructed in 2005 as part of an overall redevelopment of the ground designed by the architects Danish Siddiqui and Naval Khanna and built by a government company, Engineers Projects India Limited. Unusually, no government or other funding was involved, all the finance being raised from selling signage rights, hospitality boxes and naming rights to companies; for example Tata and ITC each have an end named after them.

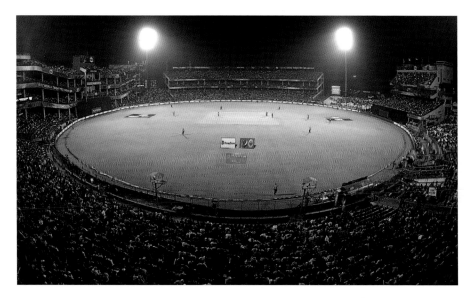

Once the cricket gets under way, the atmosphere is vibrant and engaged. Spectators describe it as 'electrifying' and 'a fabulous sporting experience'. Over the years they have seen many fine performances. Anil Kumble's match-winning second-innings analysis of 10 for 74 against Pakistan in 1999 possibly ranks highest, only the second bowler, after Jim Laker, to take all 10 wickets in a Test innings. The game almost did not take place because of a threat by radical right-wing party, Shiv Sena, to release venomous snakes in the outfield. Indian cricket writer Prem Panicker reported that the BCCI (Board of Control for Cricket in India) responded to the threat by hiring 30 snake-charmers to be in attendance just in case.

Home to: Delhi Capitals

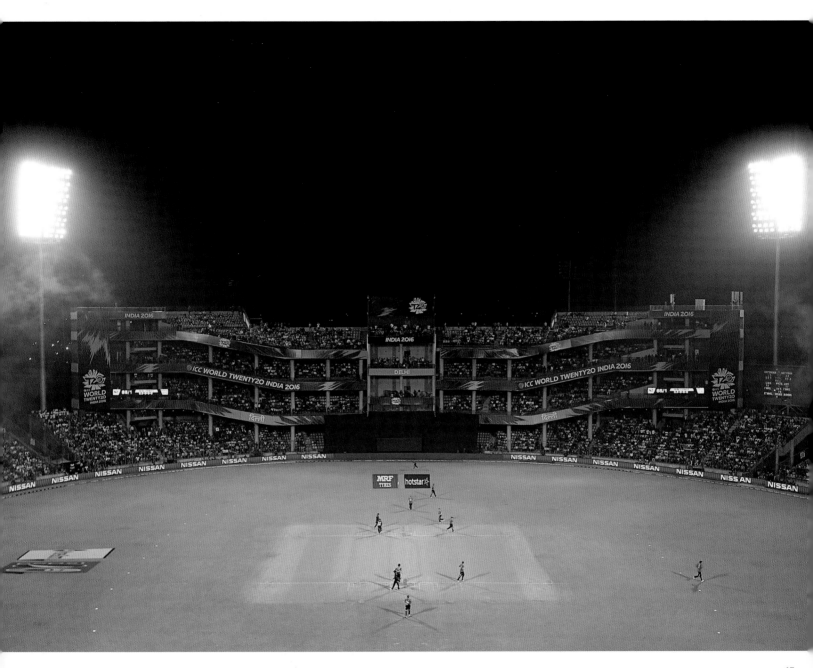

Fitz Park

Keswick, Cumbria, England

At the foot of Latrigg and Skiddaw in the heart of the Lake District National Park, overlooked by other impressive fells including Grisedale Pike, Walla Crag, Cat Bells and Helvellyn, lies one of the 'official' loveliest cricket grounds in the UK. Flanked on the town side by the River Greta, Fitz Park is home to Keswick Cricket Club, which plays its fixtures in the Premier Division of the North Lancashire and Cumbria Cricket League, while the club's second and third elevens compete in the Eden Valley Cricket League.

Cricket has been played at Fitz Park since the mid-1880s but the club ground first came to national prominence in 2001. The now-defunct *Wisden Cricket Monthly* magazine ran a competition to find the loveliest cricket ground in the country and the serious contenders were whittled down from a shortlist of 30 to six finalists. Keswick was the winner and the pavilion bears a plaque to commemorate the event.

The editor of *Wisden* magazine, Stephen Fay, described the ground as 'the most sublime backdrop you could ever imagine for a game of cricket in England'. Fitz Park is owned by trustees on behalf of Keswick Town Council. The club is not charged rental but is responsible for the upkeep of the ground and the pavilion. International cricketers such as Darren Gough, 'Hansie' Cronje and David Boon appeared in benefit matches at the ground at a time when funds were being raised for a new pavilion. Minor Counties fixtures involving Cumberland County Cricket Club have also been staged at Fitz Park. Over the years the club has employed a number of professionals, most recently the Sri Lankan Geeth Kumara who, apart from playing for the first eleven, also coaches junior players and teams.

This beautiful location suffered very badly from the impact of Storm Desmond in December 2015 when the River Greta overflowed. The ground was flooded for the first time in its history and 700 tonnes of silt were eventually removed. The pavilion, built in 1995, needed total refurbishment. The members of the club rallied round to begin the task of restoring Fitz Park to its former loveliness with the help of an ECB (England and Wales Cricket Board) grant for flood recovery, and play was back under way in 2016. Cricket standards in the Cumbria Cricket League are so high that the League is currently applying to the ECB to become an ECB accredited premier league. Keswick CC is going through a detailed process to ensure it meets all its requirements.

Home to: Keswick Cricket Club

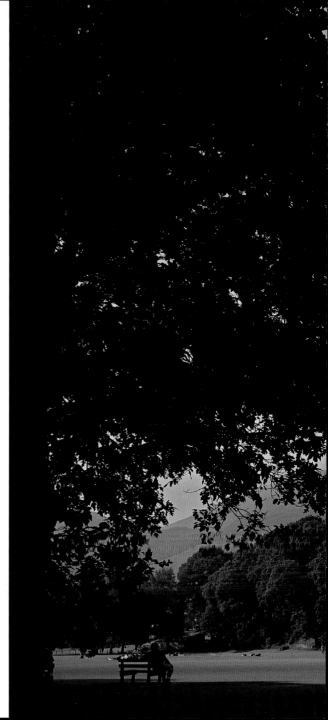

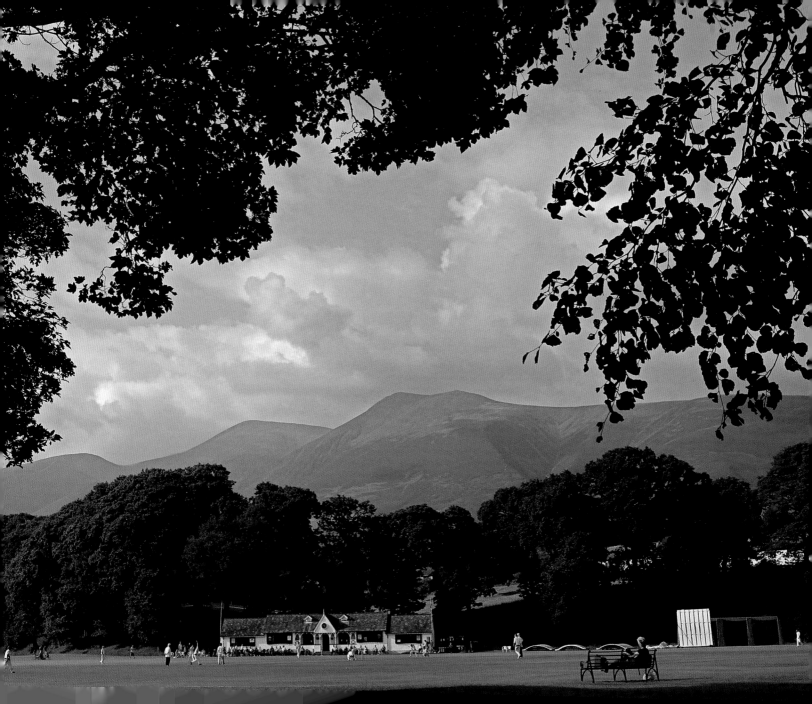

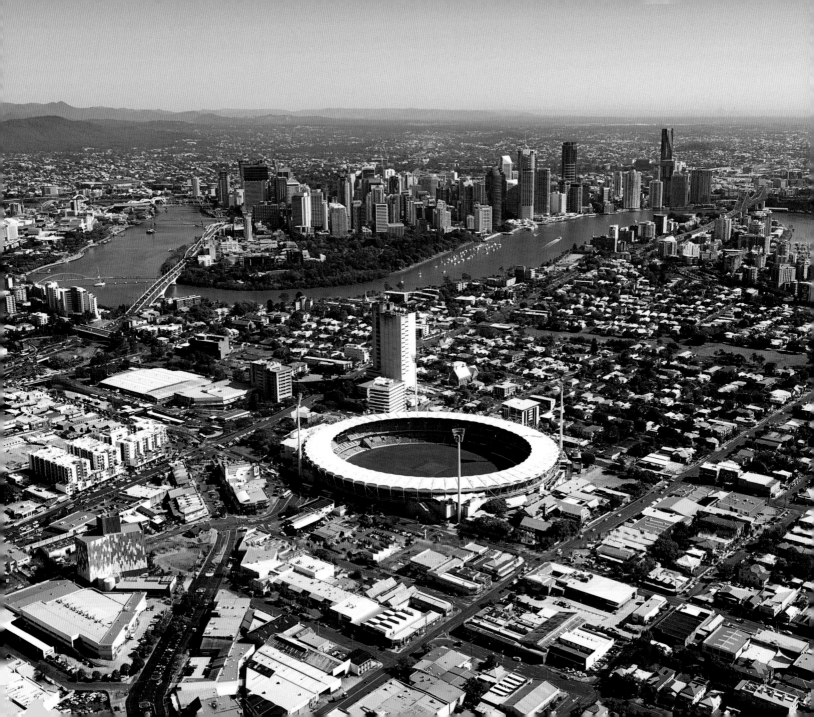

The Gabba

Brisbane, Queensland, Australia

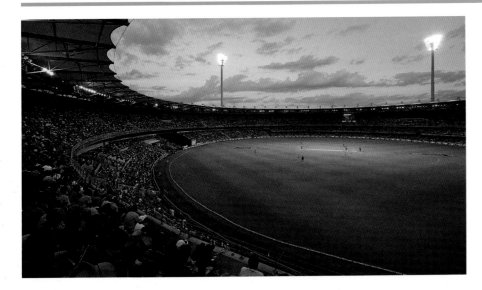

'The Gabba' is short for Woolloongabba, a suburb in the east coast city of Brisbane. No one is quite sure what the name means but suggestions are 'whirling water' or 'fight talk place'. The latter has one or two elements appropriate to an Aussie Test side.

The first match on the ground was in 1895 and Test cricket has been played here since 1931. One of the most famous Test matches of all time took place here in 1960 when Australia under Richie Benaud tied with Sir Frank Worrell's West Indies team, the first of only two occasions that this has happened.

The Gabba is famous for its fast and bouncy pitches. Opposing batmen who may not have had much pre-Test practice – the norm these days – and who seldom come across this kind of pitch anyway, seem to be found out fairly quickly.

Surprisingly there seems a certain lack of confidence about the future of Test cricket at the venue. The former Australian Test player Dean Jones pointed out that, except for Ashes games, Test match attendance at the 36,000-capacity ground was disappointing. Jones thought the stadium lacked atmosphere and, more recently, Cricket Australia has encouraged the Gabba to stay competitive with other stadiums, although to the less critical eye the stadium looks magnificent with perfect sightlines. This veiled warning comes despite the massive redevelopment which took place between 1993 and 2005 to accommodate the local Aussie Rules football side, the Brisbane Lions. Often this signals a change to drop-in pitches, but the Gabba vehemently rejected the idea in 2005, one of two major Test grounds to do so – SCG is the other. The management argues that the weather and the difference in performance means they prefer to prepare the ground in the tried-and-tested way.

As battlelines are drawn between the traditionalists and the modernists, a serious suggestion has been made to preserve the pitch with a heritage listing, although the Queensland Heritage Council seems to have thought the idea a little whimsical. As with so many renovated grounds, some of the best-loved features, such as the Gabba hill, have disappeared and some of its characters along with them. Happily, Brisbaners definitely have an appetite for cricket: the Brisbane Heat, playing in the Big Bash, draw very satisfactory attendances, but, Test cricket less so.

Perhaps the most famous game here was India's victory by 3 wickets in January 2021 to win the final match and clinch the 4-Test series 2-1. This was the series in which they had been bowled out for their lowest Test score, 36, and were missing Virat Kohli and many Test regulars. Given Australia hadn't lost at the ground since 1988 and 329-7 was the highest 4th-innings score at The Gabba, it was an astonishing achievement.

Home to: Queensland Bulls, Brisbane Heat

Galle International Stadium

Galle, Sri Lanka

Galle, situated on the coast beside the Indian Ocean, is certainly one of the most remarkable grounds in this book. On Boxing Day 2004, a powerful tsunami struck the area with devastating force as a game between Harrow School from England and a local side was about to start. One of the Harrow side reported how his team bus was swept up and deposited on the outfield. Everyone ran for the pavilion and took shelter on the balcony. Thousands of lives were lost locally and enormous damage done. The ground was reduced to rubble and the outfield became a temporary shelter for survivors.

In the aftermath, new building regulations were introduced and there was talk of relocating the ground further inland to minimise future risks, making it unlikely that it would reopen. Then somehow the regulations eased and with the encouragement of cricket luminaries such as Shane Warne and Ian Botham, and with support from around the world, Galle reopened with a match against England in 2007.

Integral to the charm of the ground is the beautiful 16th-century Old Dutch Fort. The fort, a UNESCO World Heritage site, was so solidly constructed it was able to withstand the force of the tsunami and provide a shelter which saved many lives. According to Sambit Bal, editor of ESPN Cricinfo, 'there is no better place to watch cricket from than the ramparts of the Galle Fort', as evidenced by the Barmy Army below.

Galle, which has a ground capacity of 35,000, has hosted Test cricket since 1998. If the tsunami was its lowest point, it has some highs to compensate. The holder of the world record for most Test wickets, Sri Lanka's Muttiah Muralitharan, took his 800th and final Test wicket here in 2010. Galle seems to have suited Muralitharan because he also took his 400th wicket here and 87 in all on this ground.

Home to: Galle Cricket Club

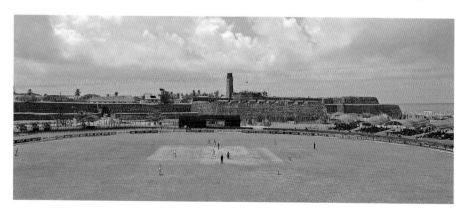

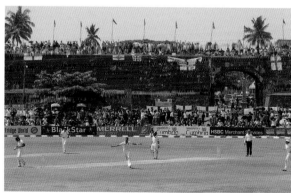

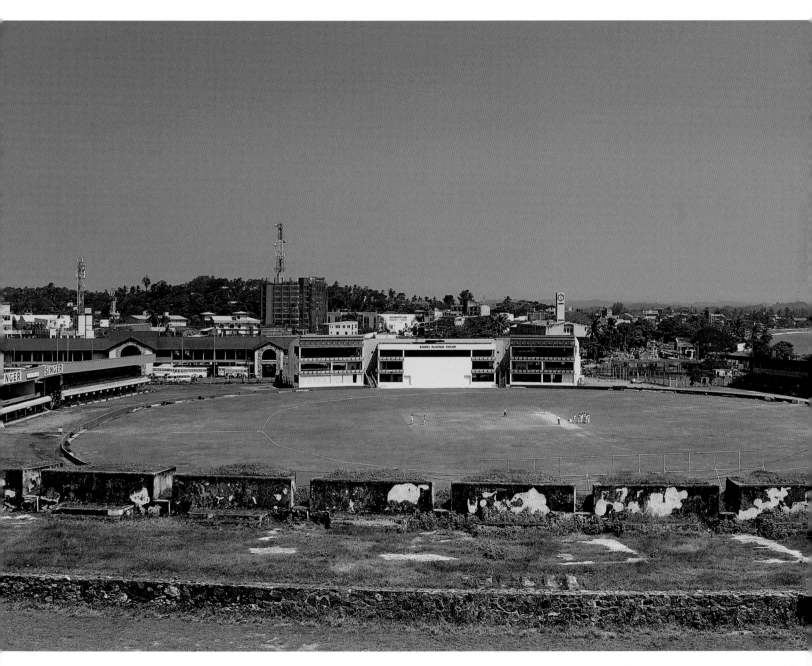

Hagley Oval

Hagley Park, Christchurch, New Zealand

Hagley Oval is set in beautiful surroundings in the centre of the city of Christchurch, very close to the prize-winning Christchurch Botanic Gardens and the leisurely flow of the Avon River. The area was settled by the British in 1850 and a cricket club formed only a few months later. The first recorded senior match took place in 1867 when Canterbury – the regional province – played Otago.

For much of its existence, Hagley Oval took second place to nearby Lancaster Park, one of the cathedrals of All-Black rugby and also the city's premier cricket stadium. From 1930 to 2006, Lancaster Park was the venue for 40 Tests, but then fell out of favour. Eventually it had to be abandoned as a sporting location following the 6.3-magnitude earthquake in February 2011. Lancaster Park and large parts of the city were devastated, including Christchurch Cathedral which had survived four previous earthquakes. Over 1,200 buildings had to be demolished.

Unfortunately but inevitably, Lancaster Park lost all seven matches it had been allocated in that year's Rugby World Cup. As it was also the main cricket arena, it seemed unlikely that Christchurch would be able to host games in the 2015 Cricket World Cup either. But Cricket Canterbury applied for fixtures anyway and, after a controversial legal process, in August 2013 Hagley Oval was chosen as the replacement site for cricket. Permission for redevelopment was granted but various legal restrictions were imposed, among them: not more than 13 match days to be allocated to major fixtures in any one season; no more than two fixtures exceeding 12,000 spectators scheduled in any three-year period; and the light headframes to be removed at the end of each season. These numbers were increased in 2019 to attract more 'top-tier' matches. The development was on a modest scale suited to its locale and the budget. Sir Richard Hadlee, generally regarded as New Zealand's greatest cricketer, opened the new Hadlee Pavilion in September 2014, a tent-like structure similar to those at Lord's and Adelaide.

Subsequently, the ground was awarded the honour of the opening match of the 2015 World Cup, an emotional occasion. Capacity was expanded to 18,000 with the approval of the court. The year before, Hagley Oval's first Test match took place in front of a full house of 7,000 when New Zealand played Sri Lanka. The home side won by eight wickets with the New Zealand captain Brendon McCullum failing by only five runs to record his fourth Test double century of the calendar year.

In 2016 the ground's second Test was played against Australia. It was memorable for widely different reasons. On the first day, McCullum hit a 54-ball century, the fastest in Test history. On Day Three, the mood was more subdued in recognition of the fifth anniversary of the earthquake, acknowledged respectfully by both teams and by the completion of one stage of the nearby Canterbury Earthquake Memorial.

Home to: Canterbury cricket team

BELOW: As well as the Hagley Oval, Hagley Park contains netball courts, a golf course and the opportunity for a leisurely punt along the Avon River which flows through the Botanical Gardens.

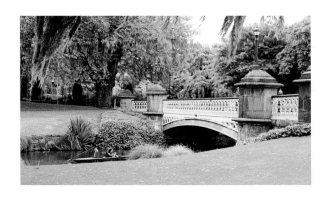

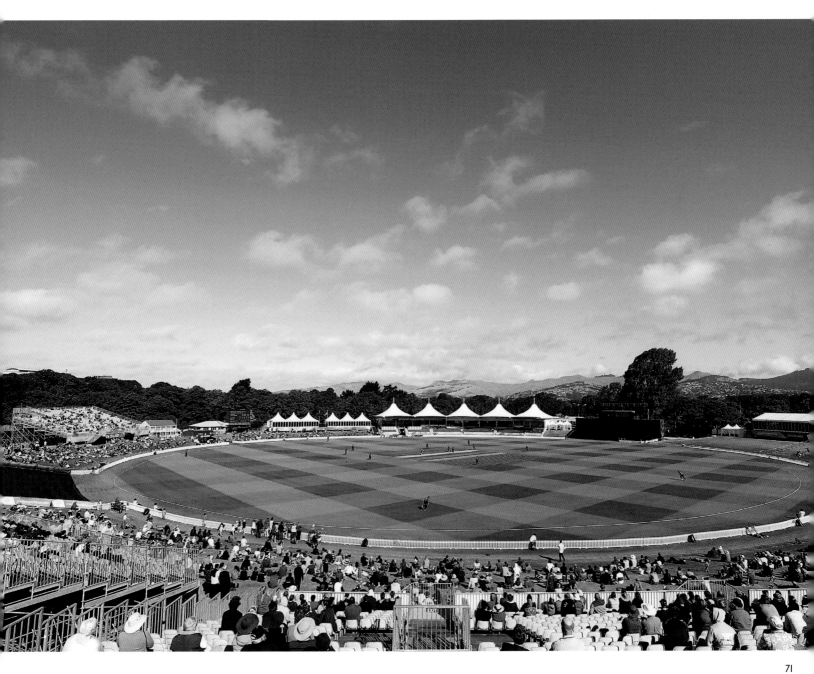

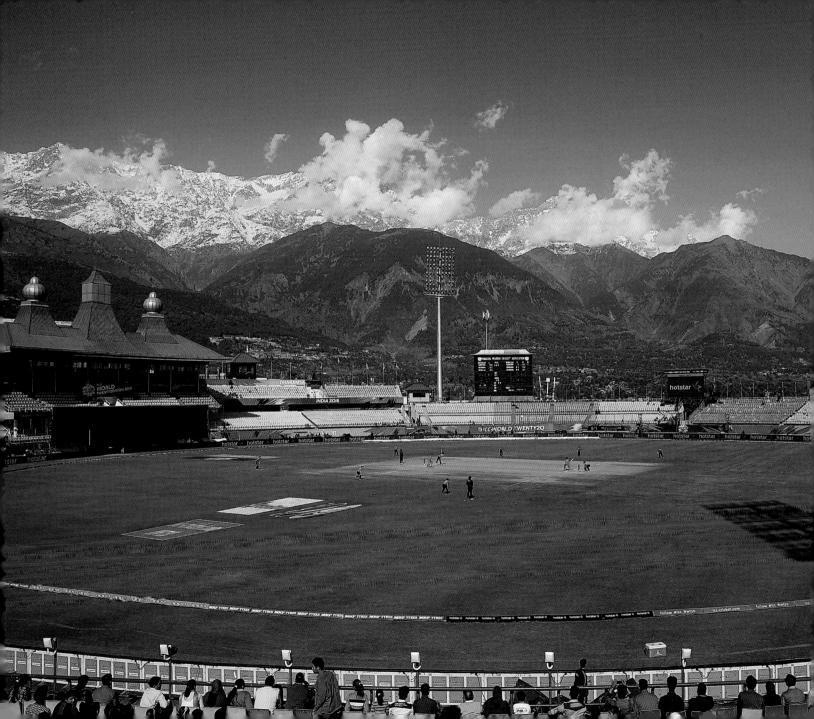

Himachal Pradesh Cricket Association (HPCA) Stadium

Dharamshala, India

A trip to Dharamshala requires a little more planning than your average visit to a cricket venue. According to the Australian journalist Geoff Lemon, who was on his way to attend a game between India and Pakistan in the 2016 Twenty20 World Cup, the drive from Chandigarh airport took all night across unpaved sections of road and the bus 'lurched and thumped with the grace of a foraging pachyderm'.

But the effort is worth it, as Lemon agreed. No one who goes to the Dharamshala stadium fails to have his or her breath taken away by the beauty and grandeur of the Dhauladhar mountains, part of the Himalayas, which overlook the ground. Peaks in the area climb to over 5,600 metres (18,370 feet) and are frequently capped with snow. Even professional cricket journalists find themselves staring at the mountains, rather than the cricket.

Entering the ground, the stunning red pagoda pavilion stands out immediately. Not so obvious is that the playing area is a perfect oval, like the one drawn freehand by the Italian master Giotto and sent to the Pope. Despite the high Himalayan backdrop, the grounds' two ends have a distinctly English county cricket feel: College End and River End. Although unlike Taunton and Chelmsford the river here is the Chandrabhaga.

The ground itself, at 1,457 metres (4,780 feet) above sea level, is the highest international ground in the world. In the days of the Raj, the British used Dharamshala as a summer hideaway from the heat. The altitude and the cold present problems for the groundsman but the use of winter rye grass prevents the grass dying off. The thin air is a boon for seam bowlers because the ball travels faster. Local knowledge advises batting second because of the evening dew.

ODIs have been held at the ground since 2013 and it hosted several games in the 2016 Twenty20 World Cup. However, an India-Pakistan game was transferred at short notice to Eden Gardens because of controversial security concerns – a big blow to the local tourist industry – and a couple more matches were rained off. Better news for the stadium, capacity about 23,000, is that it has been cleared to hold Test matches and hosted India v. Australia in 2017.

Home to: Himachal Pradesh Cricket Team

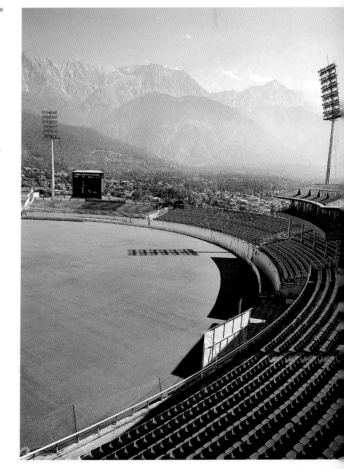

Hong Kong Cricket Club

Hong Kong, China

In a city of skyscrapers where land is at a premium, the children at one school practise cricket on the flat roof of a high-rise building. This is Hong Kong, where cricket was first played around 1841 and the Hong Kong Cricket Club was founded in 1851. Hong Kong CC is the oldest club in Asia.

The club played inter-port matches against Shanghai in 1866 and in Ceylon (now Sri Lanka) in 1890. Two years later, in 1892, the SS *Bokhara*, carrying the Hong Kong cricket team back from Shanghai, was sunk by a typhoon and 125 people died. The boat was wrecked on the Pescadores Islands and only two of the 13 Hong Kong cricketers survived.

In the mid-1970s Hong Kong Cricket Club moved from the Chater Road ground, in the business district of Victoria, to a ground overlooking Happy Valley Racecourse. The current ground, at Wong Nai Chung Gap, is in the middle of Hong Kong Island. There is a British feel to the pavilion and the club has a Long Room in the tradition of Lord's Cricket Ground. MCC teams touring Australia and New Zealand often called in on Hong Kong for a match against the ex-pats living on the island.

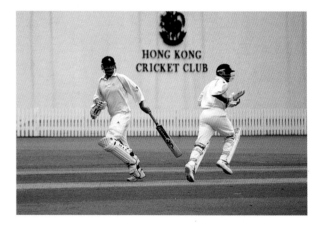

The Hong Kong Cricket Sixes began in December 1961, organised by the Hong Kong Cricket League, and it became a popular tournament for professional cricketers. In the mid-1990s, Dermot Reeve, who had been born in Hong Kong, captained a successful Cricket Sixes team. The event became a Sky Sports TV series in the 21st century.

In 1983 a team from Hong Kong played three matches in Beijing, the first time since World War II. In 1994 a Hong Kong CC team visited Shanghai and cricket was restored to the city when the team's president, Terry 'Smudger' Smith, bowled the first ball in 46 years of Communist rule. The Hong Kong international cricket team became an associate member of the International Cricket Council in 1969 and the side beat Bangladesh at a World Twenty20 tournament in 2014.

HKCC maintains strong links with MCC and former England captain Mike Gatting, in his capacity as a Patron of the club and Chair of the MCC's World Cricket Committee, visited with an MCC touring team in 2017.

Home to: Hong Kong Cricket Club

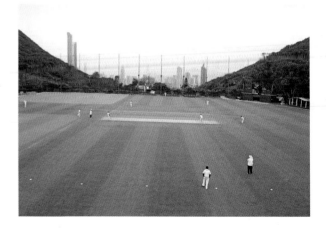

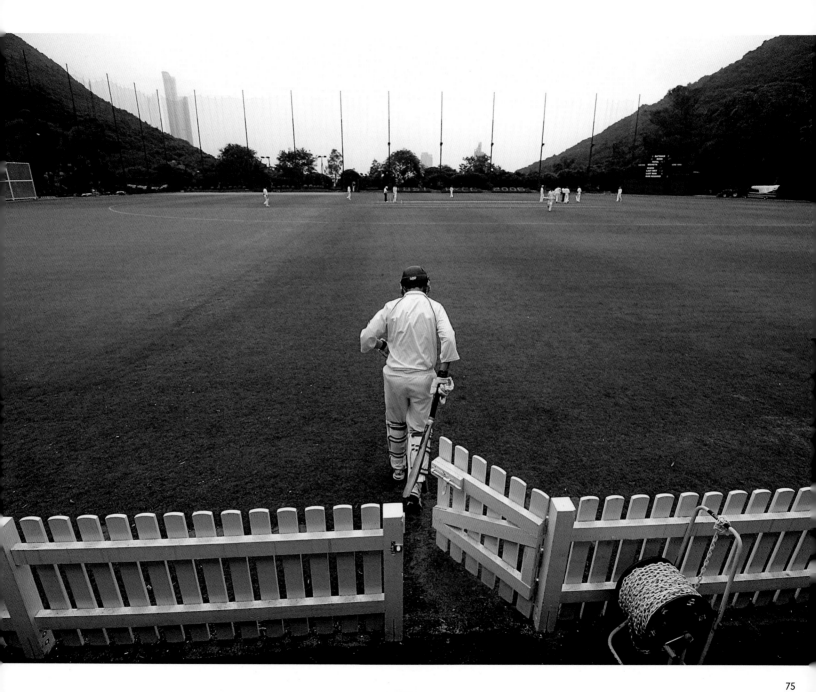

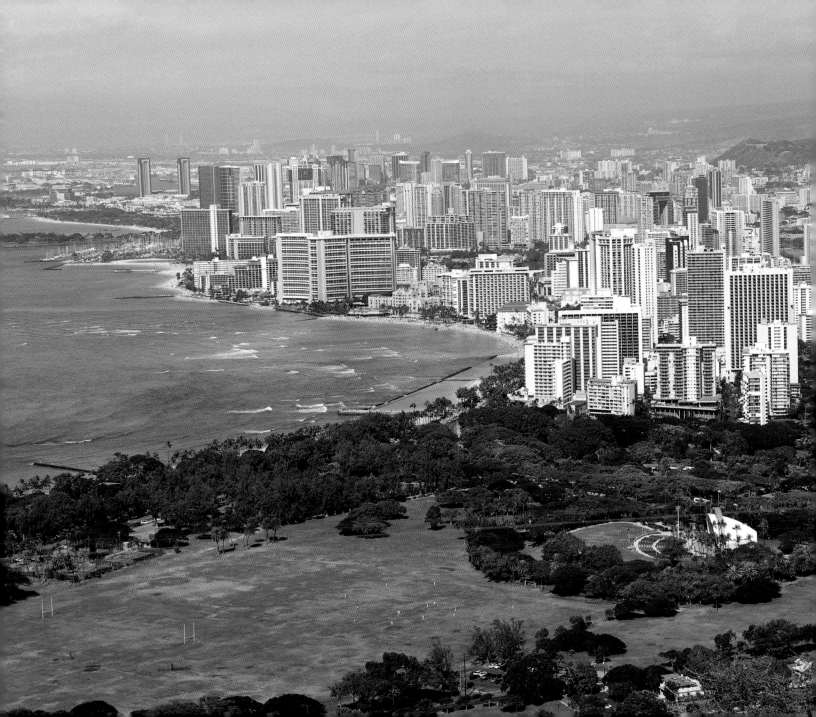

Kapiolani Park

Honolulu, Oahu Island, Hawaii

In May 1893 two of the foremost cricketers of the Honolulu Cricket Club, Mr Auerbach and Mr Weedon, wrote to the Minister of the Interior of Hawaii enquiring whether they might use an abandoned baseball ground in the shadow of the Diamond Head crater for their cricket matches.

The reply in standard officialese said yes, the Minister cordially granted them the use of the ground for practice and play. They could also take over the run-down baseball stand if they wished, including using it for 'dressing rooms, keeper's room etc'. The Board would also gladly allow them use of the sprinkler. But no, there wouldn't be any money for fence repairs.

With this permission, the Honolulu Cricket Club was established, becoming in the process, the oldest sporting organisation in the Pacific, as authenticated by the Guinness Book of Records. Cricket itself had become established in the mid-19th century under the patronage of King Kamehameha IV, surprisingly for a game which has never really taken on with the indigenous population. Players today are most likely to be drawn from cricket-loving countries such as South Africa, Trinidad, New Zealand, India and Pakistan.

According to Honolulu CC, cricket was the king's favourite sport 'and he would often practise his skills on the grounds of the Palace'. A political motive for his interest can't be ruled out as a devotion to cricket aligned his country more closely to the United Kingdom, a policy he favoured. The state flag of Hawaii still carries the Union Jack in its corner. Whatever the reason, matches involving English ships putting in to the Sandwich Islands (as James Cook named them) were being reported in local publications as early as 1847.

Cricket eventually spread to some of the other islands, such as Maui and the Big Island of Hawaii, although there were no inter-island games because it would have necessitated travel by ship. Maui CC and Honolulu CC play each other frequently today, but opponents are mostly touring sides from Australia, New Zealand and Canada, as well as visiting navies. Because of the benign weather, cricket can be played all the year round. The matting wicket needs less maintenance than a grass one, which is just as well as there is a very active Twenty20 competition.

Originally called Makiki, Kapiolani Park is named after Queen Kapiolani, queen consort of King David Kalakaua, ruler of the islands from 1874 to 1891, and an honoured guest at Queen Victoria's 50th Jubilee celebration in 1887. The dominant landmark is the Diamond Head, so named by British sailors in the 19th century who mistook calcite crystals on the beach for diamonds. It is a magnificent backdrop for the cricket and overlooks very popular surfing beaches with majestic ironwood trees providing graceful cover for visitors.

Elsewhere in the park, the Waikiki Shell is home to concerts and nearby is the Honolulu Zoo. The park began life as a racecourse and these days cricket is just one of its many sporting activities including tennis, football, lacrosse, rugby and archery. Even baseball has made a comeback.

Home to: Honolulu Cricket Club

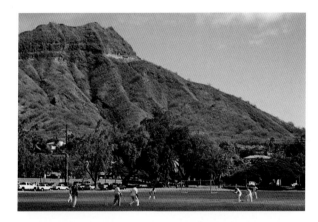

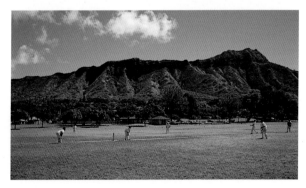

Kia Oval

Kennington, London, England

If Lord's is the 'Home of Cricket', then the Kia Oval, known as the Oval to everyone except the marketing men and women, can claim to be the birthplace of cricket's most renowned contest, the Ashes.

How the ground got its name had nothing to do with cricket, but came from the oval shape of a road surrounding a nearby market garden. When the venture failed, the Prince of Wales, who owned the land, permitted Surrey to use it for cricket from 1845. The Prince of Wales' feathers in the club's crest are a reminder of that link. A few years later in 1851, it is said that only Prince Albert prevented the land being developed for housing because he had taken a liking to the game.

The history of cricket at the Oval, certainly in the early years, is at least equal to Lord's.

In 1868 the first overseas cricket tour took place here when an Aboriginal team visited England for a 47-game tour, with the first match taking place at the Oval in front of a crowd of 20,000.

The Oval was also the scene of the first-ever Test match on English soil in September 1880 with W.G. Grace scoring a century on debut. Two years later, also at the Oval, a match took place against Australia which England unexpectedly lost. An obituary was published in *The Sporting Times* proclaiming that English cricket had died and that 'the body will be cremated and the ashes taken to Australia'. The rest is history.

The ground has so many other firsts it quite puts Lord's in the shade. It staged the first FA Cup Final in 1872, also England's first

soccer international against Scotland in 1873, also the first England v. Wales and England v. Scotland rugby internationals in England and the first Varsity match in 1877. Another little-known first is that the Oval was probably the first sports arena anywhere to use artificial lighting. According to Andrew Ward in *Cricket's Strangest Matches*, it grew so dark during a match between Surrey and Yorkshire in 1889 that gas-lamps were lit around the ground.

The Oval has witnessed many historic matches and individual feats. Sir Len Hutton scored a record-breaking 364 against Bradman's Australians in 1938. It was here in 1948 that the great Don was bowled second ball by Eric Hollies and narrowly failed to raise his Test average to 100. In 1953 Denis Compton scored the boundary that meant

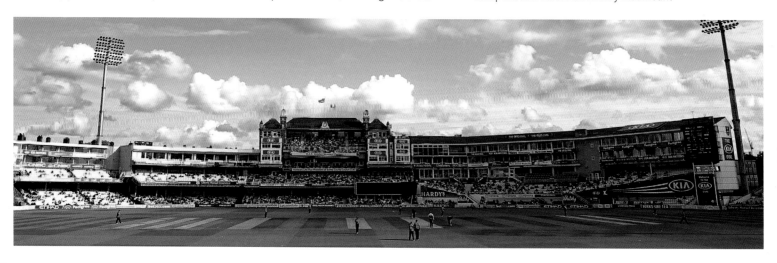

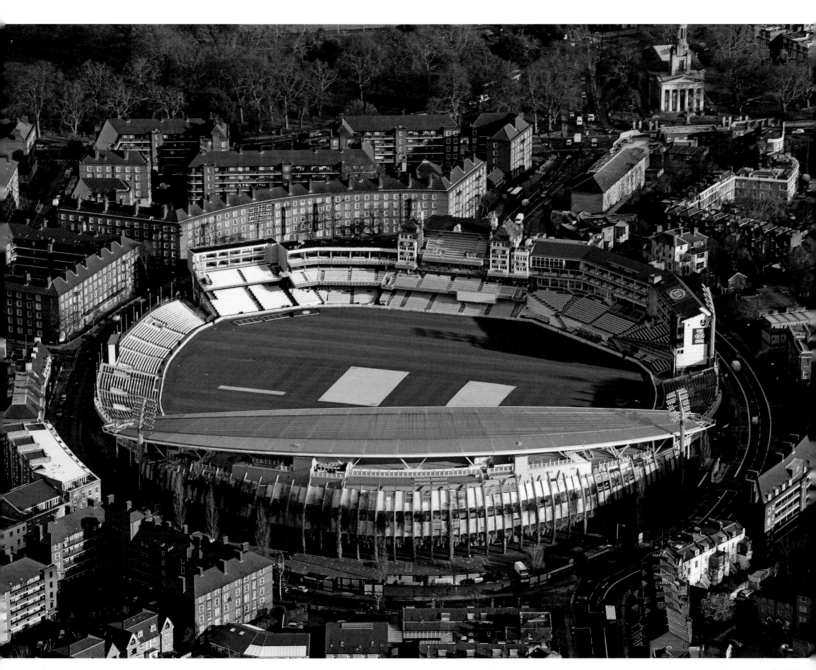

England had regained the Ashes for the first time in seven attempts. Wartime saw the ground requisitioned as a prisoner-of-war camp for enemy parachutists, though in the event they never dropped in.

The ground has been constantly upgraded in recent years and now has a capacity of 25,500 (though the target is to increase that to 40,000 in time for the 2023 Ashes series). The OCS stand, which replaces those dedicated to former players Surridge, Fender, Jardine and May, stretches from side to side of the ground in one impressive span. Built over the course of two years, from 2003 to 2005, the new stand increased capacity by 4,000. It also provided new conference facilities and business rooms. The stand seating is demountable, allowing different configurations depending on the sight screen locations. Externally, a 'living wall' of vines and creepers softens the impact of the stand for local residents.

Another new stand replaces the Lock, Laker and Peter May stands and has a hotel backing on to it. The Victorian pavilion, dating back to 1898, has been impressively upgraded with a new entrance. Some of this development has impinged on the playing area so that the Oval no longer ranks as highly as it once did among the world's largest playing areas.

More than many grounds, the Oval seems to have a definite personality. Perhaps this is due to the famous but redundant gasholders just outside the Oval's walls which date back to the mid-19th century. When they were decommissioned in 2013, the cricketing world, which treasured them, held its breath. It was possible that they might be torn down, as in other parts of the country, and the land developed into housing. In the event, in 2016 they were protected when Historic England granted them Grade II listed status.

Perhaps the Oval's unique appeal is also due to cricket commentator Henry Blofeld rhapsodising about the buses 'going down the Harleyford Road', or maybe to the exuberant West Indies supporters who noisily cheered on their country in its cricketing prime during the 1970s and 80s, or simply to the cricket fans who take their drinks up to precarious-looking positions on the roofs of nearby buildings and enjoy themselves with a free day at the cricket.

Home to: Surrey County Cricket Club

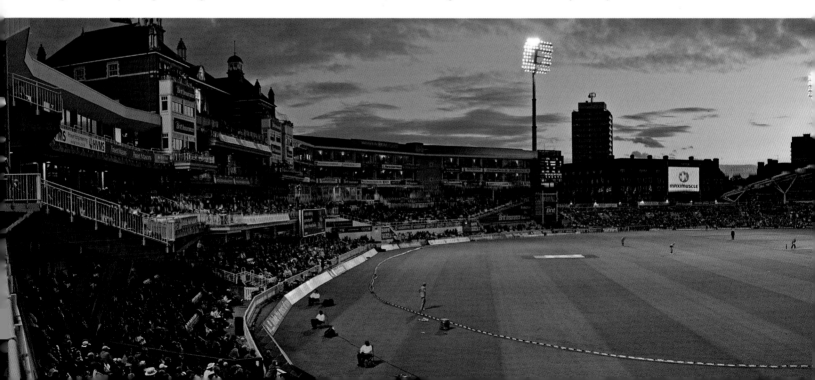

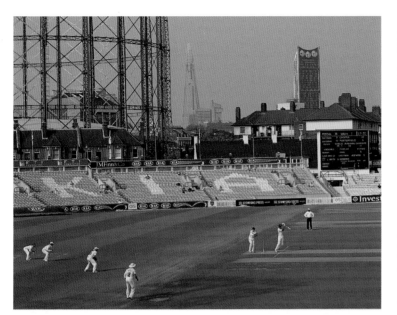
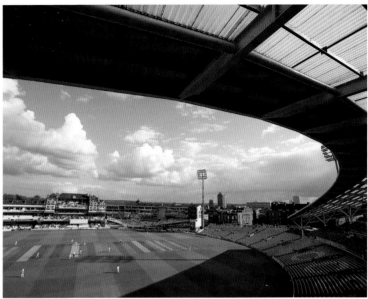
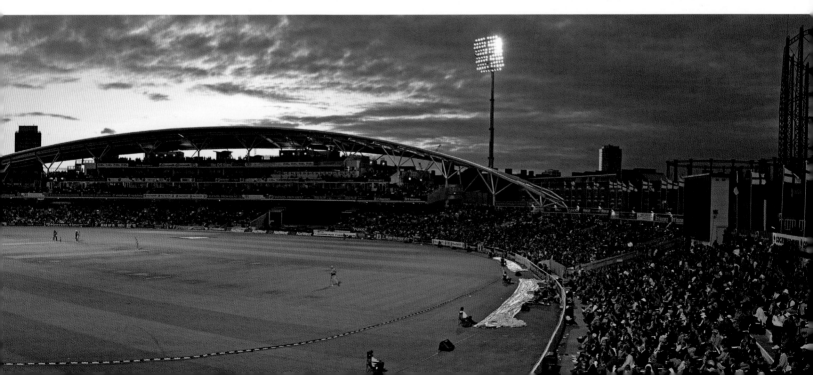

Lake St Moritz

St Moritz, Switzerland

Once a year towards the end of February, a group of ardent cricket lovers will put on their whites and venture out onto a frozen lake in front of the promenade at St Moritz, the famous Swiss ski resort. Over the course of a weekend, four English and Swiss teams will play a round-robin tournament of three games per team. Apparently, back in 1988 the snow failed to appear and rather than twiddle their thumbs, someone had the bright idea of playing a game of cricket. Golf, horse racing and ice polo were already thriving, so maybe imitation was the sincerest form of flattery. One way or the other, Cricket on Ice was born.

Participation is by invitation only, but there are no onerous tests of cricket skills and players are of varying abilities, from novice to quality cricketers. The idea is to give all a chance to participate while still trying to win the game. Umpires generally enter into this spirit too.

Rules are largely the same as a normal Twenty20 game, although a rubber/plastic indoor ball is used, as a normal cricket ball becomes wet and heavy. Sight screens are dispensed with, as the background is deemed white enough. A ball may bounce twice on its way to the batsman, more than that and it's a no-ball, as is failing to land on the matting pitch. As a concession to the conditions, gloves and sunglasses are permitted. Interestingly, the rules also specify that members of the media may be tolerated on the field during play.

The St Moritz club has a very limited fixture list and relies on guest players, who have included former England Test stars, David Gower and Gladstone Small. The St Moritz Tourist Board takes a keen interest and helps out with the lake infrastructure and some financial backing. A little luxury is heating inside the tents, courtesy of a sponsor.

The social aspect of the weekend is important, according to the organisers. In an incident which made the papers, Gower left his hired car on the lake overnight while he enjoyed an evening's conviviality, perhaps at the tournament's black-tie gala dinner. Returning in the morning, he found the vehicle had sunk to the bottom of the lake, an incident which cost him 20,000 Swiss francs.

Games can be followed on the ECN (European Cricket Network) channel on ECN YouTube. A team score between 140 and 150 will normally win you the match. Individual scores over 50 are unusual but not unknown.

Home to: St Moritz Cricket Club

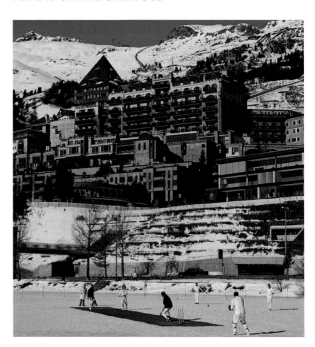

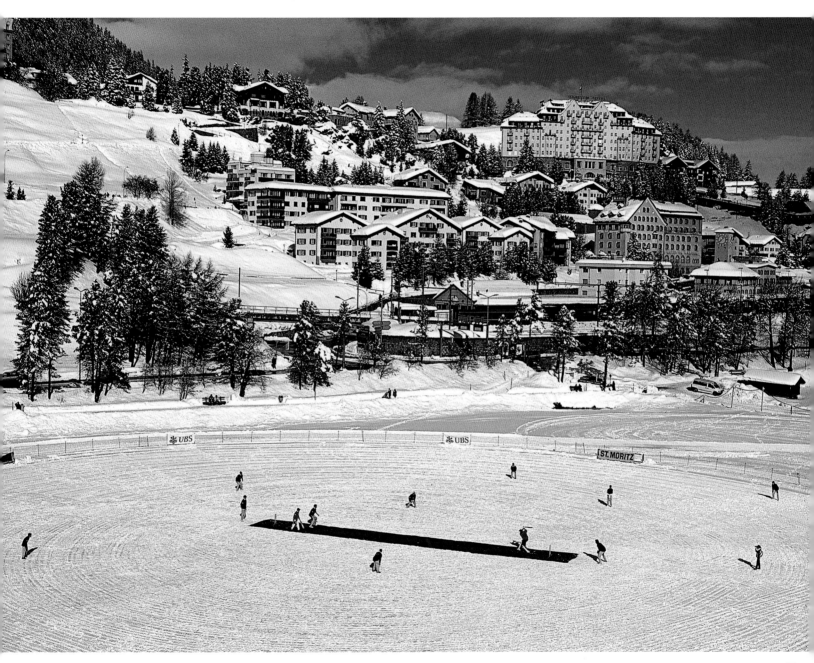

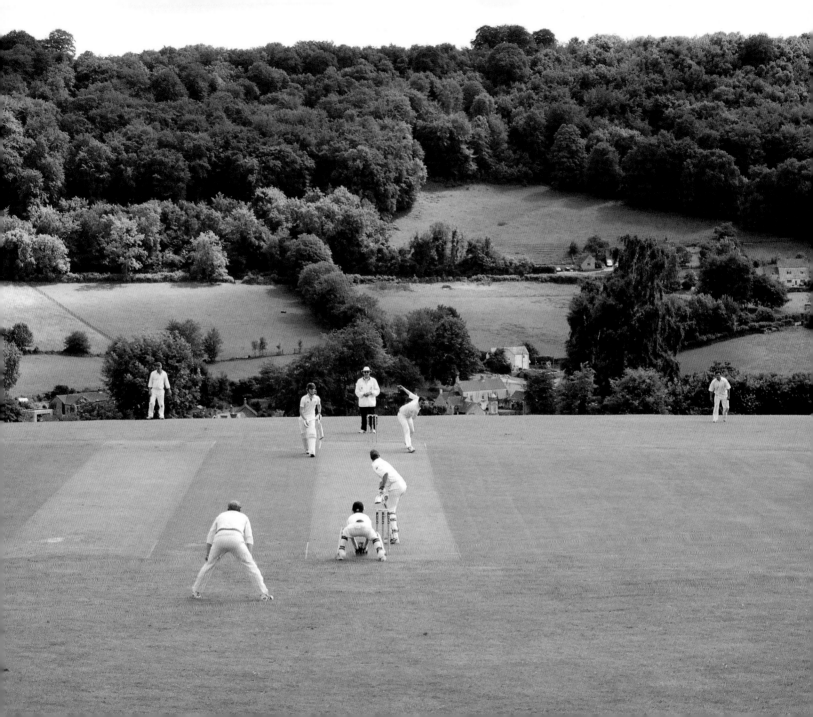

Laurie Lee Field

Sheepscombe, Gloucestershire, England

Sheepscombe Cricket Club is inextricably linked with the poet Laurie Lee, probably best known for *Cider with Rosie*, the first volume of an autobiographical trilogy. For many years Lee allowed the club free use of a field he owned in Sheepscombe, now called the Laurie Lee Field.

The ground is idiosyncratic in the best traditions of English village cricket. There is a huge drop of 4.6 metres (15 feet) from the pavilion side to the boundary on the other side. It plateaus enough to provide a flat pitch area more or less in the middle. The bowler's run up from one end is so steep that shorter batsmen can't see him till the last few strides. The home side knows to alert fielders and shout a warning if a catch or groundstroke is on its way. Boundaries are a lot easier to earn on the downward slope. A six up the hill towards the pavilion has been achieved but it's a rarity. Lee wrote affectionately of his Uncle Sid who learned his cricket 'on the molehills of Sheepscombe', which is not far from characterising the ground today. It is all very English and reminiscent of A.G. Macdonell's famous chapter about country cricket in *England, Their England*.

Lee's sympathy towards cricket remained even after a disquieting experience at Sydney Cricket Ground. He was watching a game from the notorious 'Hill' when he was hit by a flying beer bottle. After four stitches in hospital, he said of the experience, 'I enjoyed it, but if I go back again I will wear a tin hat.' Lee died in 1997, but is still remembered with warmth at Sheepscombe. After his death, the club bought the ground from his estate with help from the England and Wales Cricket Trust, and from a very supportive local community. In celebrating the purchase, the club unveiled a fine bench overlooking the pitch in his memory.

The club, founded in 1896, play in the Gloucester County Cricket League, which includes teams with wonderful names like Hawkesbury Upton and Aston Ingham. The traditional pavilion has been significantly upgraded since 2015 and the youth section goes from strength to strength. It is good to know that with hard work from the players and supporters, the club is thriving and has no problem recruiting new players.

Home to: Sheepscombe Cricket Club

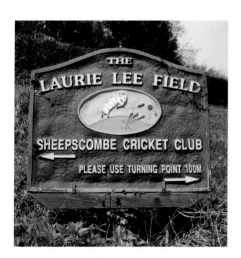

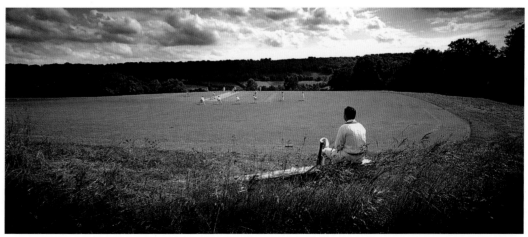

Lord Braybrooke's Ground

Audley End House, Saffron Walden, Essex, England

Audley End House, the beautiful mansion that stands serenely in the heart of the grounds, now belongs to English Heritage. Over the centuries, it has reflected many of the twists and turns of English history. Originally dating back to the Norman era, in the 16th century it was a Benedictine abbey. In the 17th century it was rebuilt on a scale so palatial that Charles II bought it for £50,000 as a base for attending Newmarket races.

Subsequent owners cut it down to the scale it is today. Towards the middle of the 18th century it passed to the Braybrooke family, who owned it until 1948. It is thanks to them that the local cricket club can enjoy the use of one of the most lovely settings in English cricket, designed by, among others, renowned landscape architect Capability Brown.

Cricket has a long history at Audley End. The MCC visited regularly in the 19th century and surprising names turn up. In 1848 one of the Audley End team was none other than John Wisden. He took five wickets in the second innings in a game which the Audley End team, mainly made up from estate workers, won by 61 runs.

In 1948, when the Lord Braybrooke of his day decided to hand over his property to English Heritage, he made it a condition that the club should continue to use the ground rent-free. English Heritage did not quibble but insisted that the club should play its games on the far side of the river Granta, which runs calmly through the park. There is only one ground rule: balls going into the river earn six runs even if they bounce first.

Today Audley End plays in Division 1(S) of the Cambridge League (though potentially looking to merge with nearby village Wendens Ambo) on a wicket described as slow. Visiting teams are very keen to sample the ultra-English atmosphere and the home team finds itself playing a good number of friendlies. A visiting side from Australia once insisted on playing for the 'Ashes' and club president Bill Starr only found a suitable facsimile at the very last minute. The house has many interesting period features and exhibits and its amicable relations with the club side extend to challenging it to a game of cricket. The catch was that the game had to be played with curved Georgian bats and old-style wickets with only two stumps, and in Georgian clothing from the house's extensive collection.

Home to: Audley End and Littlebury Cricket Club

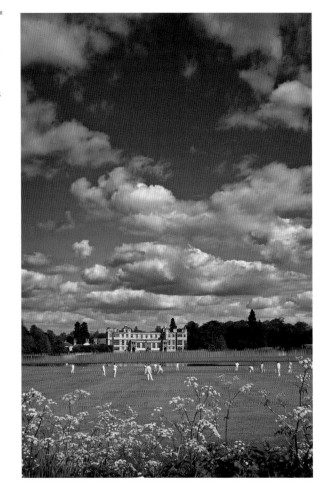

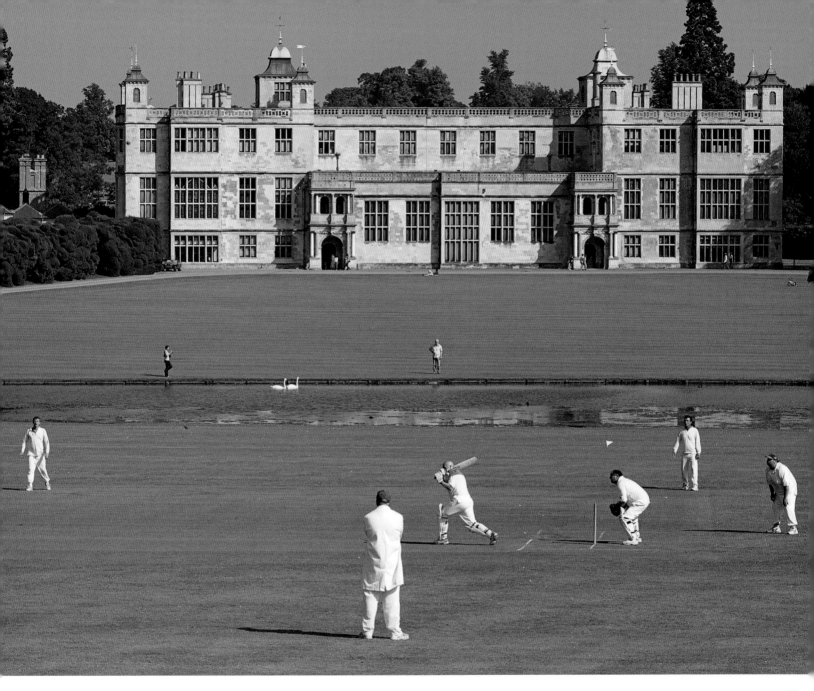

Lord's

St John's Wood, London, England

The magnificent Lord's Cricket Ground has gone through several metamorphoses. The ground is named for Thomas Lord (1755-1832), a good bowler but a better entrepreneur. Asked by the Earl of Winchilsea and the Duke of Richmond to find a new venue for the well-known White Conduit Club, Lord found them a ground in Dorset Square, Marylebone, known as Lord's Old Ground.

Following a rent dispute, he relocated to a new venue known as Lord's Middle Ground, but after a couple of years was forced to move again when the government requisitioned the area in order to build the Regent's Canal – a plaque on the bridge commemorates the event. Lord then moved to the present site in busy St John's Wood in 1814, apparently taking all his turf with him. When he ran into financial problems, he was bought out by William Ward, an accomplished cricketer and director of the Bank of England. So today's site is the third ground, though maybe it should be Ward's, not Lord's.

Today the playing area is immaculate, but a head groundsman of the 19th century, William Slatter, recalled sheep grazing on the match ground, making holes with their feet that remained for the rest of the season. One of Lord's most famous features is its slope, which aids the more skilful bowlers. Slatter records a drop of 2 metres (6.6 feet), though

today it is reckoned at 2.4 metres (8.1 feet). The weather vane on the roof of the Mound Stand, showing Father Time removing the bails from a wicket, is another well-known image. The one object that should not be missed is that most iconic of all cricket memorabilia, the Ashes Urn, located in the Lord's Museum, itself the world's oldest sporting museum. Awarded to the winner of Test series between England and Australia, the winner receives a replica because the fragile original has only very rarely left Lord's.

Lord's has always renewed itself and developments in recent years have included the construction of new stands and a dominating media centre observing proceedings like an all-watching eye. The pavilion, built towards the end of the

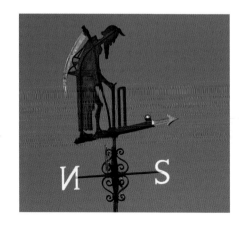

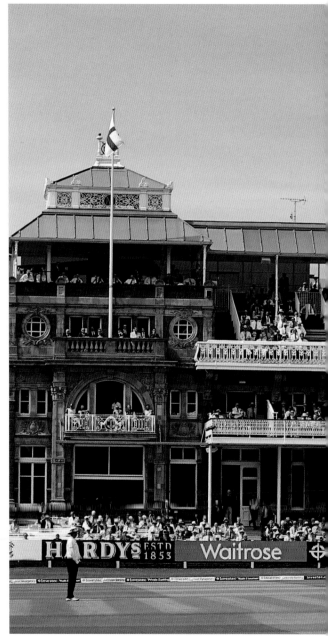

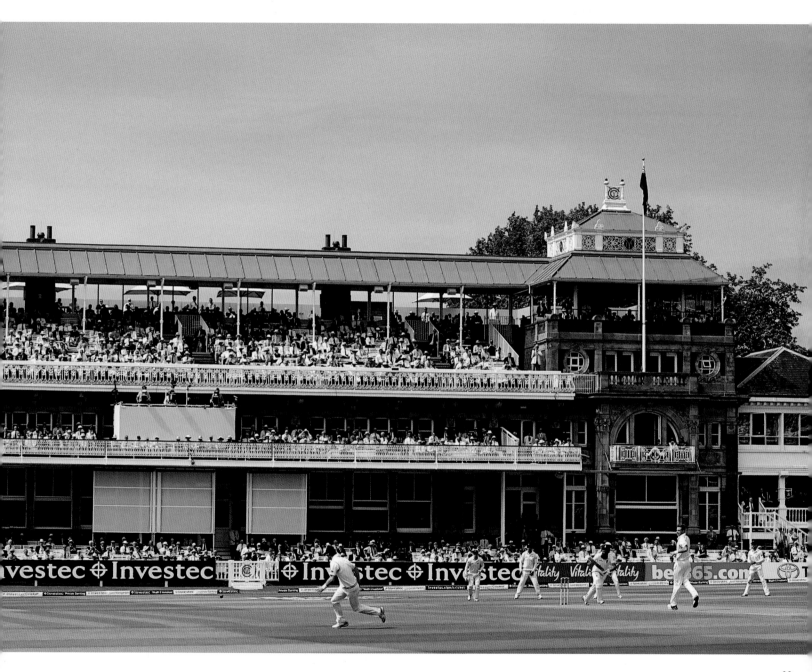

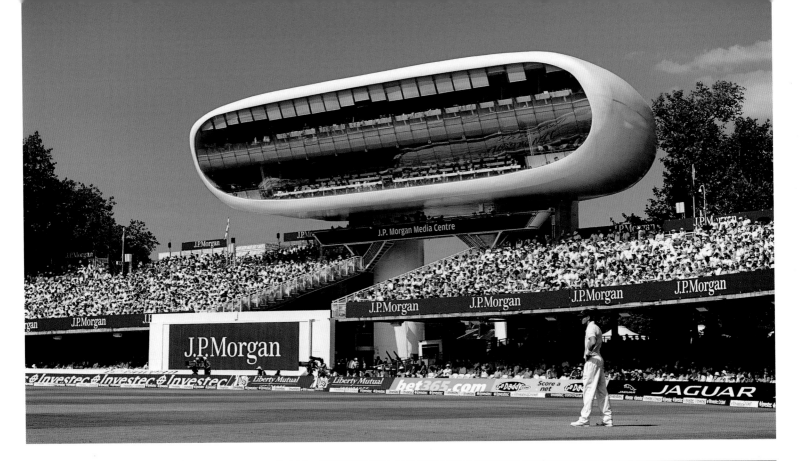

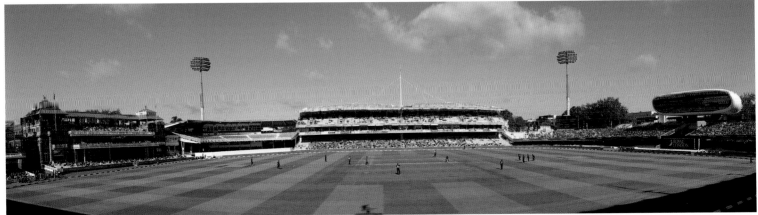

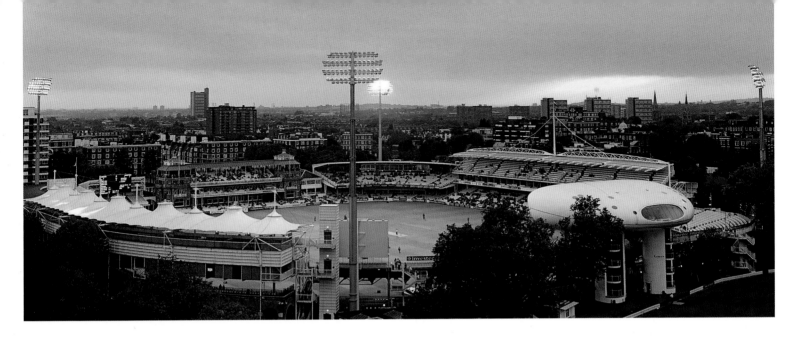

Victorian era, is protected by a Grade II* listing and remains largely unchanged on the outside, although the inside is constantly refurbished. MCC say they are determined 'to continue to own the finest cricket ground in the world', but the competition is fierce, as this book shows. No one disputes that Lord's provided a matchless venue for the archery competition in the 2012 Summer Olympics.

All this costs money and MCC sometimes sells off a little of the family silver to raise the cash. In November 2010, the Lord's Library sold *Cricket: A Collection of All the Grand Matches of Cricket Played in England from 1771 to 1791* by William Epps, a book so rare that not even the British Library had a copy. A buyer paid the then-world-record price of £151,250. In case it was on your reading list, don't worry, it was the library's spare.

The future includes the building of two new stands which will raise the capacity from

the current 28,000 to 30,530, still a long way behind in the table of largest grounds. It will no doubt remain as hard as ever to get a ticket for Tests.

Lord's has moments in its history it would prefer to forget, ranging from the match-fixing gambler Lord Frederick Beauclerk in the 1830s to the disgraced American financier Allen Stanford, who landed there in a helicopter in 2008 with $20 million dollars of dubious provenance to finance a rival Twenty20 league to the IPL.

But most cricket lovers will forgive such blemishes. Lord's is the Home of Cricket and the premier Test ground in the world where every cricketer longs to play. Anyone lucky enough to walk through the Long Room and down the steps of the distinctive pavilion will follow in the footsteps of the most illustrious cricketers of all time, including W.G. Grace, Bradman, Tendulkar, Vivian Richards,

Botham, Lara, Warne and many others.

In 2019 Lords was the scene of the most exciting one-day cricket final of all time when England won the Cricket World Cup Final beating New Zealand. After each side had batted the scores were level. A Super Over was played and the scores were still tied. England were declared the winners having scored more boundaries in the game.

In 2020, due to the pandemic, Lord's came perilously close to not hosting any games for the first time since 1787 when cricket was played at Lord's Old Ground. Eventually a new 4-day county competition, the Bob Willis Trophy, was inaugurated. Lord's was the venue for the final between Essex and Somerset in late September but without spectators. There was no international cricket at the ground for the first time since 1970.

Home to: Middlesex County Cricket Club

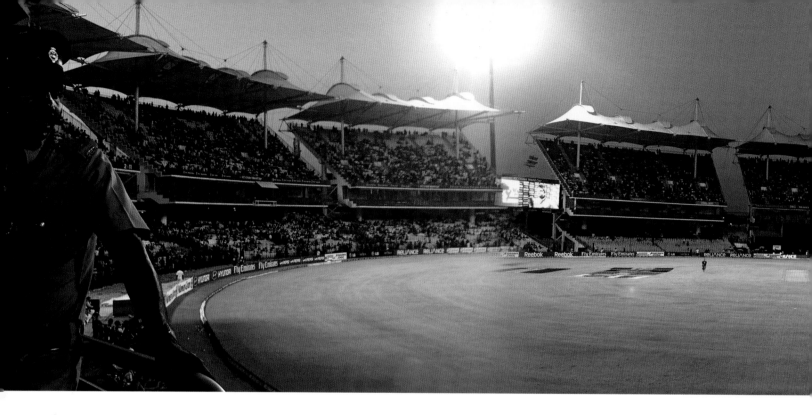

M.A. Chidambaram Stadium

Chepauk, Chennai, India

In 2009 Hopkins Architects were presented with an unusual design specification as they planned the redevelopment of Chepauk, the more familiar name for the M.A. Chidambaram Stadium. Well-known for designing the Tavern and Mound stands at Lord's and Hampshire CCC's Ageas Bowl Stadium, Hopkins were directed, in cricketing parlance, 'to get our swing back'.

Until the construction of the existing stadium in the 1970s, the ground had been famous for the help it gave swing bowling, created by the incoming sea-breeze from the nearby beachfront. But the 1970s construction blocked off the breeze and the administrators not to mention the swing bowlers, wanted it back. As an added unusual requirement, the architects were directed to adhere to the principles of Vastu Shastra, an Indian tradition similar to feng shui, in the design.

Hopkins met their brief with a beautiful and visually interesting ground comprising 12 separate stands. Various design features allow the breeze to flow through the gaps left for that purpose, although statistics are not yet available to assess how much this has improved the opening bowlers' figures.

With the ICC Twenty20 World Cup scheduled to take place in India in March 2016, Chepauk was selected as one of the eight host grounds. Then an unexpected obstacle occurred. The TNCA (Tamil Nadu Cricket Association), the managing body

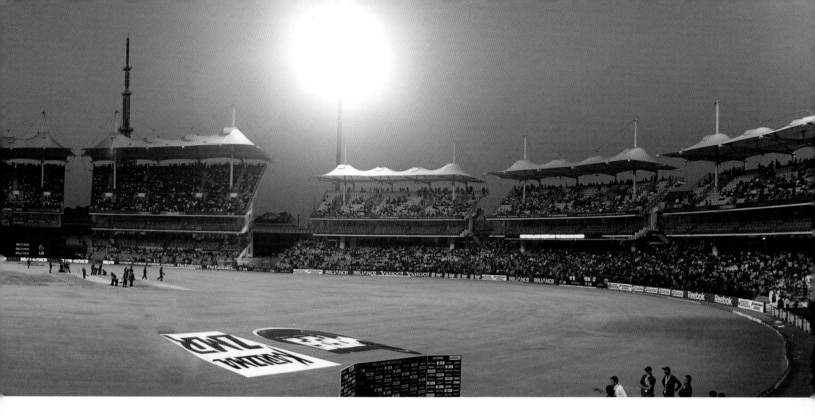

of the ground, was taken to court in a case involving the demolition of a gymnasium adjacent to three of the new stands. TNCA could not proceed with the demolition without the permission of the State's Heritage Committee as the gymnasium was considered a heritage monument. The three stands were sealed for future cricket events until the issue was resolved and the ground missed out on the opportunity to take part in what turned out to be a pulsating tournament.

This unfortunate series of events seems out of character for Chepauk. Suresh Menon, editor of *Wisden India Almanack*, has written that 'if Indian cricket has a spiritual home

it is Chepauk'. Established in 1916, it is the oldest continuously used cricket stadium in the country.

The first ever Ranji Trophy match took place here in 1934, although scheduled for three days, it was all over in one. In 1952 it was the site of India's first-ever Test victory. In 1986 the India v. Australia Test resulted in the second of the only two tied Tests in cricket history. Other statistics include Sunil Gavaskar scoring his 30th Test century in 1983 and breaking Bradman's record; Narendra Hirwani taking 16 wickets on Test debut in 1988, a record for any bowler; Virender Sehwag scoring the fastest triple century ever in 2008, 300 off 278 balls.

What seems to attract Suresh Menon and others to the ground is a warmth of spirit, epitomised by the way the crowd gave Saeed Anwar a standing ovation for his record-breaking 194 in 1997, or the applause given to Pakistan on their lap of honour after a Test victory in 1999. When it was suggested that the stadium should be relocated to the outskirts of the city for space reasons, the offer was rejected. As Menon writes, Chepauk 'is more than its records… you don't uproot a temple because you might have more parking space elsewhere'.

Home to: Tamil Nadu Cricket Team; Madras Cricket Club

Maifeld

Berlin, Germany

Of all the venues in this book, none have the disquieting historical overtones of the Maifeld, where the mass Nazi rallies of Hitler's Third Reich were held.

The Maifeld was developed in the early 1930s at the same time as the adjoining Olympic Stadium built as the centrepiece of the 1936 Olympic Games. It was a huge lawn of some 28 acres, with standing room for 250,000 and seating for 60,000, primarily intended for holding gymnastic displays and the annual May Day celebrations. In the 1936 Olympics, polo and equestrian events took place here. After the war, the area was part of the British Sector and up to 1990 was used by the British for the Queen's Birthday Parade, and for games of rugby, polo, football and cricket.

Cricket has been played in Germany since 1850 and at one point it was a popular leisure activity. At the turn of the 20th century, Berlin alone had more than 30 cricket pitches. Now it is a fringe sport with some 50 clubs across the country playing on coconut fibre and, less often, grass, under the auspices of the German Cricket Federation founded in 1988. The national team, ranked 39th in the world, takes part in the European Championships. Unsurprisingly, the football-crazy German public is blissfully unaware of the game and, according to Berlin-based writer and photographer Fabian Muir, a cricketer wishing to enjoy a bit of practice 'can be certain that before long an unassuming local will spread a towel in the centre of the pitch and lie down,' presumably mistaking it for a beach.

Most likely to be looking for a net are members of the Berlin Cricket Club. The club, founded in 1985, moved here in 2012 after some bizarre events at their previous ground at Körnerplatz. Arriving one day for a practice, they found the pitch dug up and a ban in place forbidding them to play. Officialdom said that the cricket balls were a danger to passers-by, even though it had been used for cricket since the 1950s.

The Maifeld, where they eventually moved to, comes with plenty of historical baggage, most obviously the Olympic Stadium, the dominant 77-metre (253-foot) high bell tower and the sense of the past. Facilities, according to Muir, are very good, and include sight screens, scoreboard, nets and two fields. It is generally agreed that the move has been a success and good for German cricket. A youth programme run by the Quentin-Blake-Europeschool is developing a new generation of young players. Women's cricket is well established too.

The prophet Isaiah wrote of beating 'swords into ploughshares'. In this of all places, he might have been surprised to find them beaten into cricket bats.

Home to: Berlin Cricket Club

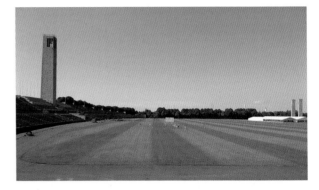

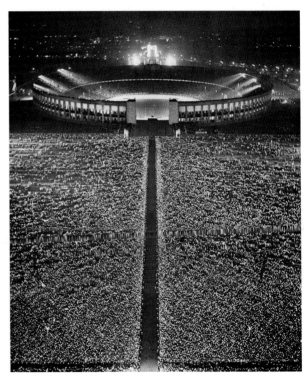

RIGHT: The opening of the 1936 Summer Olympics at the Berlin Olympic Stadium.

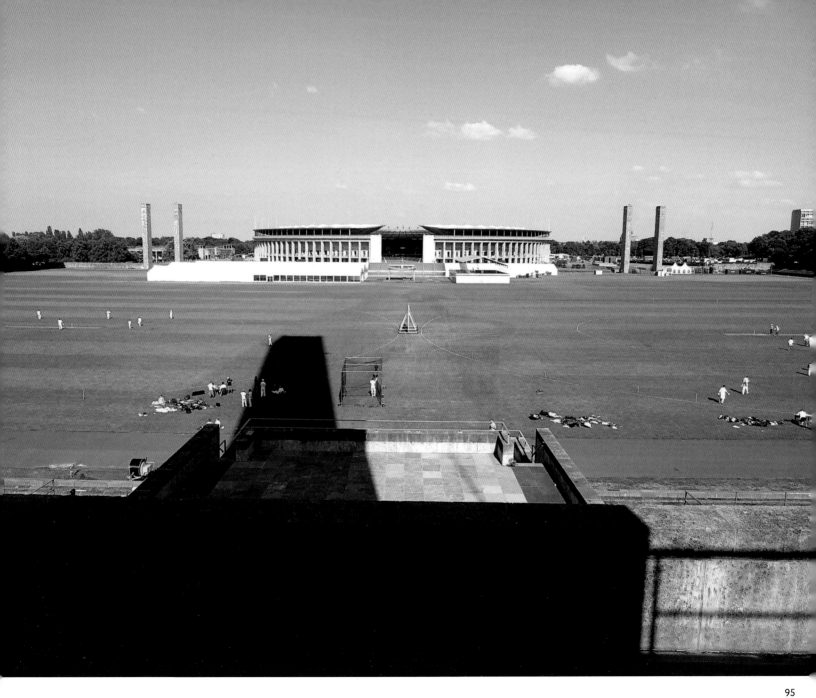

Marvel Stadium

Melbourne, Victoria, Australia

The Marvel Stadium, formerly known as the Etihad Stadium and Docklands Stadium, is remarkable in that it is the only large-scale cricketing venue with a closable roof and that roof brings its own unique problems. It is typical of a new breed of multi-purpose stadium, such as Moses Mabhida Stadium in Durban, which seemed to spring up in the first decade of the century. All are equally at home hosting a variety of sports, such as soccer, athletics, Aussie Rules football in Australia, speedway and cricket. If there's a free couple of hours, they put on a concert. Bums on seats is the mantra.

It's fun but confusing to the traditional cricket lover. The teams that play there often have names like the Sydney Sixers or Hobart Hurricanes, product of the worldwide sporting mania for alliteration.

The stadium took less than three years to build. Opening in 2000, it started out as the Victoria Stadium and in its relatively short existence has also been known as the Colonial Stadium, Telstra Dome, Etihad Stadium and now the Marvel Stadium. Unusually, the stadium is primarily designed for Aussie Rules football, rather than cricket, which has resulted in a media box located square of the wicket, which is not so good for the cricket writers.

Whatever the pros and cons for cricket, the project has taken what was previously dormant wasteland and by constructing a sophisticated new stadium, given the area

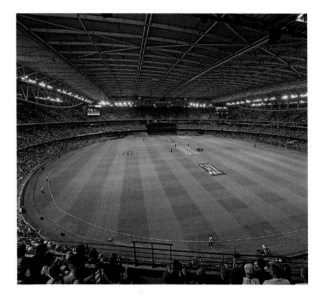

a new lease of life. The aim is to provide perfect weather-independent conditions at all times so the roof is retractable. Spot a threatening cloud and the roof can be closed in eight minutes.

With 'proper' cricket played at the MCG, cricket here is limited to the Big Bash Twenty20 League, which has a short explosive season running from mid-December to mid-January each year. The Renegades' players for the 2015–16 season included Aaron Finch, Dwayne Bravo and Chris Gayle, who hit a 12-ball half-century, equalling the fastest 50 ever. A new rule had to be introduced in 2012 when a shot by Aaron Finch hit a beam on its way up to the roof and was ruled 'dead ball'. A rule change was introduced for balls striking the infrastructure, making some shots worth six, but its application makes the Duckworth-Lewis rules look simplistic in comparison.

There is no questioning the stadium's popularity. In January 2016, 43,176 people attended the local derby against the Stars. Crowds are vast for other events too: the biggest crowd was 70,059 for a Jehovah's Witnesses convention in 2014.

Whether you like or don't like the stadium may depend on whether you like your spring flowers forced or natural. But there is no denying that it does not look out of place in Melbourne's spectacular Docklands quarter.

Home to: Melbourne Renegades

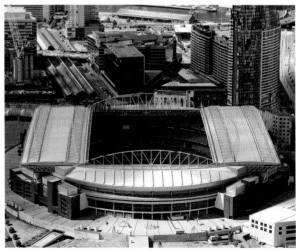

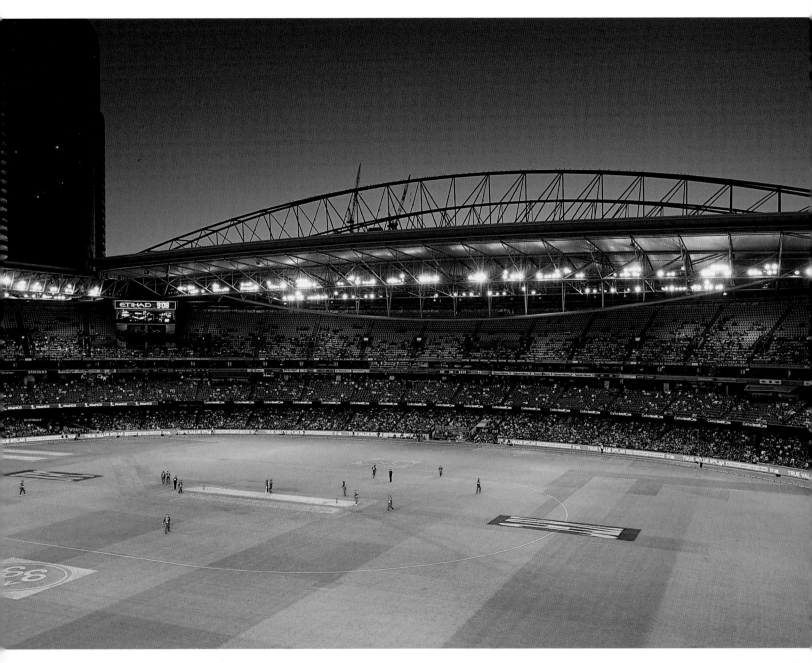

Melbourne Cricket Ground

Melbourne, Australia

A lot of excellent cricket has been played at the MCG over the years, but what takes one's breath away is the almost intimidating vastness of the stadium and the size of the crowds, with attendances sometimes exceeding 90,000.

A crowd of 93,013 attended the 2015 World Cup Final between Australia and New Zealand; 91,092 were present at the first day of the 2013 Boxing Day Ashes Test, a world record for Test cricket. Non-sporting events can attract even more, as when Billy Graham drew 130,000 to a rally in 1959. Grandstand redevelopments and health and safety legislation now limit the maximum seating capacity to approximately 95,000 with an additional 5,000 standing room capacity, bringing the total capacity to a remarkable 100,024.

The first ground on the current MCG site was built in 1853 after the Melbourne Cricket Club had moved several times following its founding in 1838. Offered three alternatives from which to select a new site by Governor La Trobe, the Lieutenant-Governor, the club selected Richmond Park, now known as Yarra Park, a site of significance to Aborigines. Use of the land was restricted to cricket only until 1933.

Over the years dozens of grandstands were expanded, pulled down or burnt down, as in 1884. With management always ambitious to upgrade and develop, by 1912 stand capacity had reached 20,000.

The 1956 Olympics also prompted further development with the construction of the Northern, or Olympic, Stand, at which point the ground's capacity had reached 120,000. By 2005, some of these stands were demolished and replaced with a single structure for the 2006 Commonwealth Games, although history was respected as the names of the old stands were retained for sections of the new facility.

Bradman loved it here, scoring nine Test centuries, more than anyone else. He particularly liked playing against England and scored 100 in each of the six Test matches against them, except the last in 1947. A famous number – 1,107 – the highest-ever total by a first-class team, was scored here by Victoria, who had also scored 1,059 against Tasmania three years earlier. The MCG celebrates its heroes and evocative statues honouring Bradman, Dennis Lillee, Keith Miller and Shane Warne among others can be found around the perimeter of the ground.

MCG will always have an honoured place in the history of cricket as the site of the first ever Test, which took place in 1877 between England and Australia. In March 1977, a commemoration match was held to celebrate the 100th anniversary of the match, and, by a quirky coincidence, Australia won by 45 runs, the exact same margin as 100 years previously.

Home to: Victoria Cricket Team

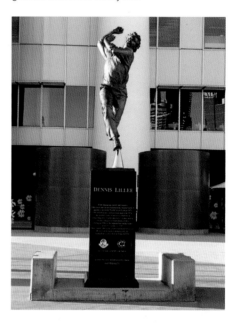

BELOW: One of MCG's statues to its cricketing legends. This one honours Dennis Lillee, 'the greatest fast bowler of any era'.

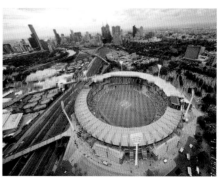

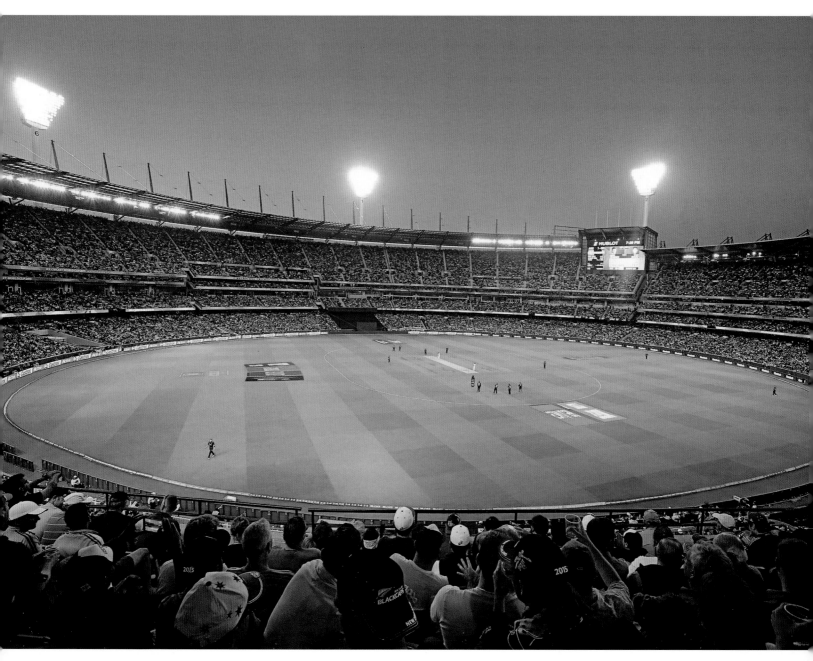

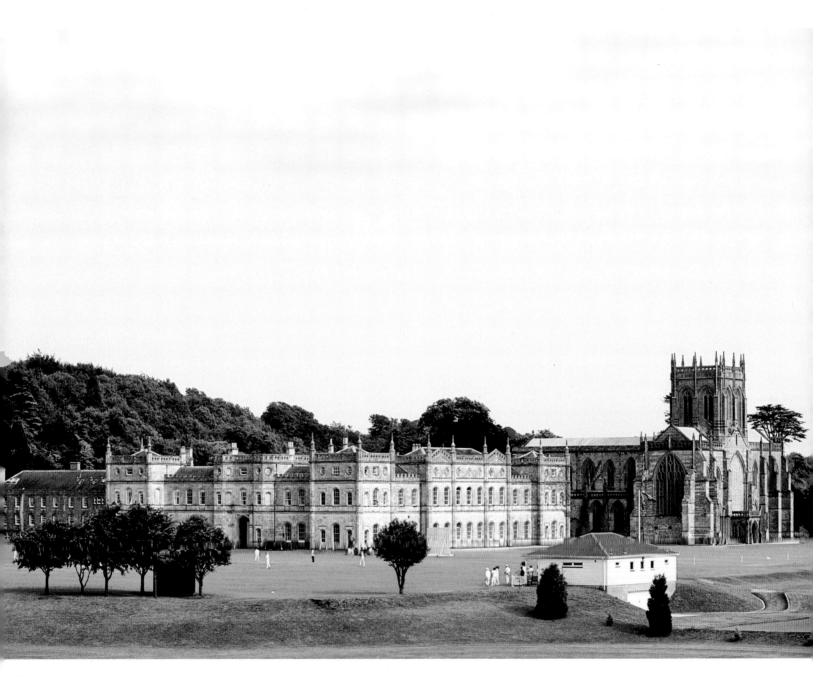

Milton Abbey School

Blandford Forum, Dorset, England

Milton Abbey stands in a confluence of valleys in the Dorset downs, near to the market town of Blandford Forum. Although the school opened relatively recently (for an English public school) in 1954, the history of the grounds it occupies is ancient and can be traced back to the 10th century. A Benedictine monastery established in 964 was destroyed by fire in 1309, although the Benedictine influence is still evident today in Milton Abbey's church, which is central to the school's ethos. Two famous names are associated with later developments of the estate – Capability Brown who designed the layout of the grounds, which are Grade II* listed, and Augustus Pugin, principal architect of the Palace of Westminster, who designed the south window of the church.

Like many such establishments, monastic life came to a halt with the dissolution of the monasteries by Henry VIII. Eventually the property came into the possession of the 1st Earl of Dorchester, who from 1780 onwards built the elegant Georgian mansion house which provides such a graceful background to the school's cricket matches.

With beautiful spacious grounds stretching for acres, looked after by a staff of six, the school has plenty of room for sports, including three cricket squares; a nine-hole golf course designed by Peter Alliss; football, rugby and hockey pitches, as well as an all-weather facility. According to *Tatler*, the rampant rabbit population is kept in check by third-formers who use ferrets to protect the main square.

The school plays regularly against the MCC, the Forty Club and other schools, and it also makes its facilities available for disability cricket. With a view to Dorset CCC playing minor counties games here, the school alumni raised funds for a £6,000 electronic scoreboard to bring it up to the necessary standard.

Home to: Milton Abbey School Cricket Team

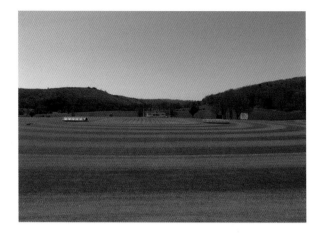

RIGHT AND BELOW: The school's extensive grounds include cricket pitches on the parklands in front of the mansion house and behind the chapel.

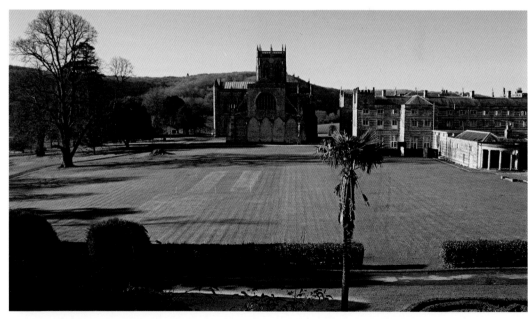

Mitcham Cricket Green

Mitcham, South London, England

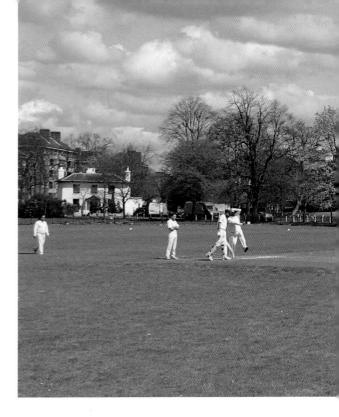

Cricket has been played at this location since before 1685 and it is generally acknowledged to be the oldest continuously used ground anywhere in existence. You would think that this longevity deserved stability but in recent years the ground's custodian, Mitcham Cricket Club, seems to be constantly living through 'interesting times'.

The club plays in the 1st Division of the Fuller's Brewery Surrey County League and also runs 2nd and 3rd XIs and a strong colts section. It is very proud of its strong links to women's cricket, which go back to 1937, as well as its friendship with the late Molly Hide, captain of the WCA England team and a respected administrator. The 1937 Surrey v. Australia women's match is reliably reported to have attracted a crowd of 10,000 spectators.

The club's pavilion arrangements are highly unusual in that the A239, a busy main road, divides the pavilion from the ground. In order to avoid situations where an incoming batsman tries to dodge his way through the traffic to get to the wicket before being timed-out, the rule is sensibly suspended for matches here.

The pavilion is a late-Victorian building and contains cricket memorabilia including paintings of former captains and photos of the team going back to 1904. However, in quite a complicated ongoing legal situation, it is not owned by the club but by a third party and there is some uncertainty about its future. Mitcham is a very heritage-conscious community with organisations dedicated to ensuring that the pavilion will not be developed in ways that will be out of keeping with its historic associations.

And there is much history to be proud of. Lord Nelson was once a spectator here, W.G. Grace played here and was run out, and Ian Botham made a guest appearance with the Queen's Jubilee Baton. A good-size memorial stone in one corner of the ground contains names of famous cricketers associated with the club, including Andrew Sandham, Herbert Strudwick, Tom Richardson and James Southerton, all of whom played for England, Surrey and Mitcham.

Southerton's Mitcham connections are particularly strong as he was the landlord of a local pub, The Cricketers, in the second half of the 19th century. Three worthwhile entries in cricket's collection of trivia relate to him. At the age of 49 years and 119 days, he was the oldest man to make his Test debut and he was the first Test cricketer to die. He was also once duped by W.G. Grace and returned to the pavilion under the false impression that he'd been out caught, the entry in the scorebook reading 'retired thinking he was out'. Thanks to a grant secured by Mitcham Cricket Green Community and Heritage, the stone was cleaned and the names of more modern eminent Mitcham cricketers were added in 2014, including Dennis Marriott (Surrey and Middlesex) and D.M. Smith (Surrey, Worcestershire and England).

Despite the uncertainty surrounding the future of its pavilion, it is clear that Mitcham intends to continue as the historic, community-conscious, cricket-loving organisation it has always been, with Julia Gault CBE at the helm.

Home to: Mitcham Cricket Club

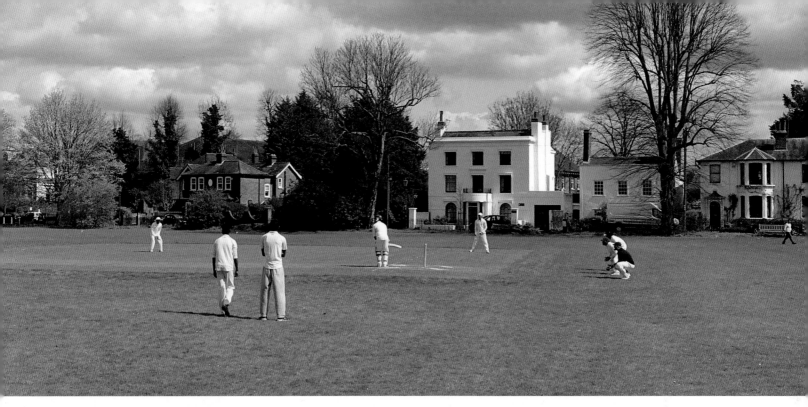

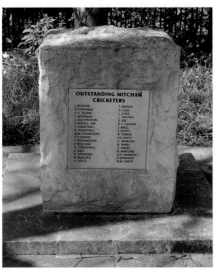

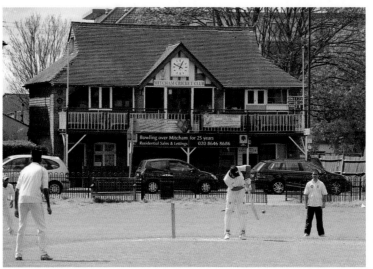

LEFT: Mitcham's pavilion lies on the other side of the A239 from the Cricket Green, but nearby traffic lights halt the flow of vehicles regularly enough to allow players across.

FAR LEFT: The memorial stone sits in a corner of the ground across the road from a Grade II-listed pub named after one of Mitcham's greatest players. Burn Bullock may not have the reputation of James Southerton, but the King's Head was renamed the Burn Bullock in his honour. Sadly, the grand building has been shuttered for several years.

Moses Mabhida Stadium

Durban, South Africa

The Twenty20 cricket match played at Moses Mabhida Stadium on January 9 2011 in front of 52,000 spectators broke records. But not of the six-hitting variety.

In win-or-lose terms the match for the Krish Mackerdhuj Trophy was a disappointment for hosts South Africa who lost to India by 21 runs. But the biggest-ever crowd for a cricket match on the African continent were not there simply to see the Proteas snatch a win. They were there to witness and celebrate the final game of the great South African paceman Makhaya Ntini ahead of his retirement. And the Moses Mabhida Stadium was a fitting venue for the great man's valedictory performance.

More than most grounds, symbolism was key in the design of Moses Mabhida Stadium. Its name memorialises one of the heroes in the struggle for a democratic South Africa. The iconic arch, 350 metres (1,148 feet) long and 106 metres (348 feet) high, runs from one end of the stadium to the other and was inspired by the Y shape of the South African flag. The two legs of the arch at the southern end become one at midpoint, representing the principal South African cultures joined together as one people. The 11 different colours of the seats represent the beaches, the sand and the colours of local natural life. The stadium, finished in 2009, has been described as a defining landmark to match

the Eiffel Tower, Sydney's Opera House or the London Eye. Visitors can take the SkyCar up to the highest point of the arch and enjoy breathtaking views over the city. With such imaginative features, it is no surprise to find the arena voted the most popular stadium in South Africa in an online poll. The ground is multi-purpose. In 2010 it hosted seven matches in the FIFA World Cup, including a semi-final. The 2022 Commonwealth Games will be held here and the ground capacity can be increased to 85,000 for major events such as the Olympics. It is also a popular venue for big-name music concerts.

The conversion from a soccer or athletics stadium into a cricket ground is not straightforward. For the first match, it took nine weeks to prepare the pitch and make sure it was level and the moisture content was right. A drop-in pitch couldn't be used because of the 2 million rand cost of shipping it in from Australia or New Zealand. The groundsman, Phil Russell, described it as the most challenging pitch he had ever prepared. However, with the crowd-drawing success of the 2016 Twenty20 World Cup in India, a South African tournament could hardly ignore the prospect of future games at such a large and remarkable arena.

Home to: South Africa National Team

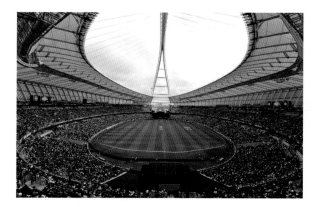

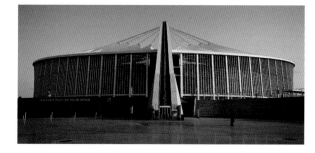

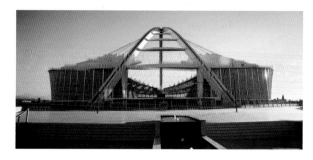

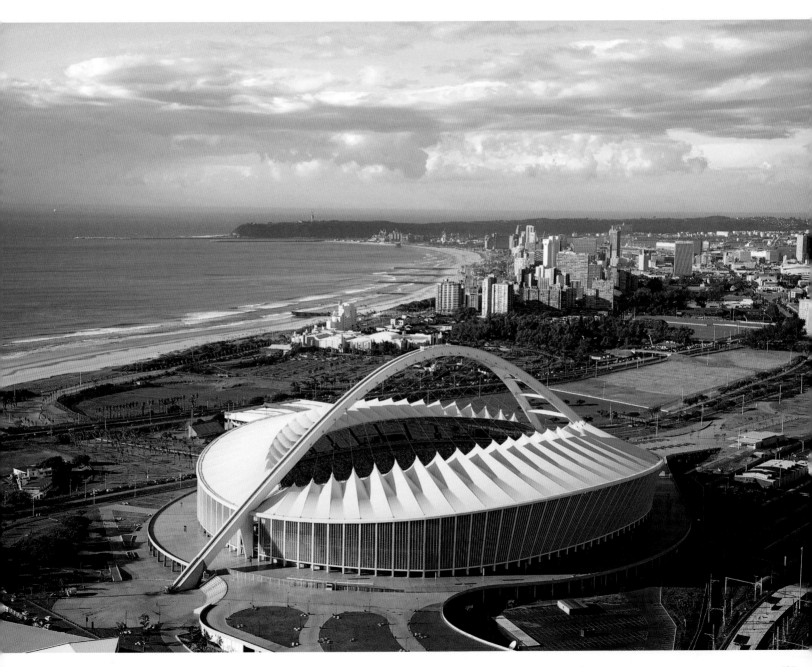

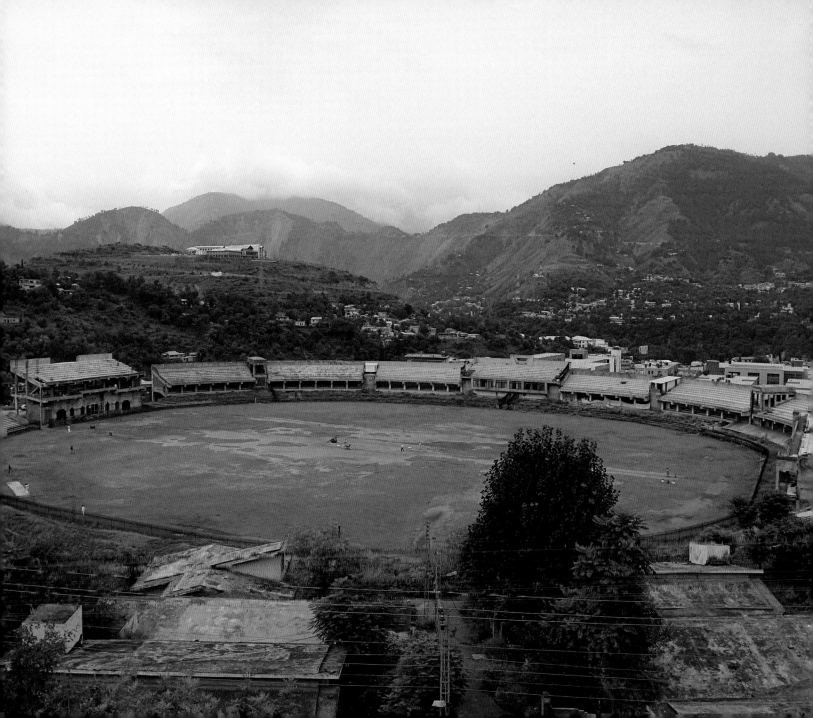

Narol Cricket Stadium

Muzaffarabad, Pakistan

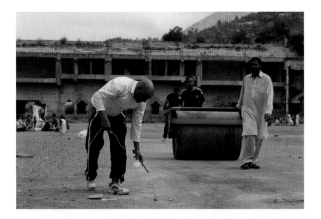

In October 2005 a devastating earthquake hit the Azad Kashmir region of north-eastern Pakistan, killing up to 80,000 people. Its impact was described by the UN Secretary-General Kofi Annan as worse than the previous year's Indonesian tsunami. In Muzaffarabad, only 64 kilometres (40 miles) from the epicentre, many of the buildings were damaged or destroyed. The main cricket centre, the Narol Cricket Stadium, didn't escape the destruction and was quickly converted into a field hospital. The once lush, green outfield rapidly filled up with victims of the disaster, as U.S. military helicopters flew in from nearby Afghanistan along with five RAF Chinooks deployed across the region.

Sport was not the first priority in the aftermath of a disaster, but just as Galle has returned to the international fold, assisted by the great and the good of the cricketing world, so Narol and its unique amphitheatre-like stadium has been resurrected as a place for cricket.

British project engineer Paul Snook, working in the Kashmir region, documented the progress of the rehabilitation of Narol over two years between 2011 and 2013. His first set of photos show the grandstands

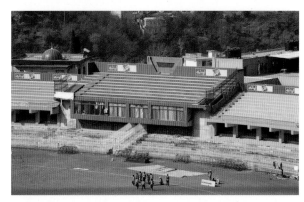

overgrown with weeds, the railings rusty and unpainted, but the groundstaff actively working on improving the playing surface.

'They brought in special termite-aerated soil from a village near Lahore,' says Snook of the playing surface being carefully rolled in his photos.

Returning two years later, he found a cricket ground that was in keeping with its beautiful surroundings. Railings and pavilions had been painted, the outfield grass had improved; it may not have been finished but the level of cricket being played was serious enough to warrant the use of Pakistan Cricket Board (PCB) umpires. Organised league and local cricket has now returned to Narol, one of the most beautiful cricket grounds on the Indian subcontinent.

Home to: Muzaffarabad Cricket Club, Narol CC

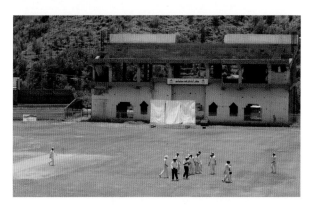

New Field

Sedbergh School, Sedbergh, Cumbria, England

The market town of Sedbergh in Cumbria developed in the 12th century at the confluence of four rivers, where ancient trade routes merged. The school is set in magnificent parkland overlooked by the mighty Howgill Fells and is also close to both the Yorkshire Dales and the eastern fells of the Lake District. It is within easy walking distance of the town centre and the Grade I listed parish church of St Andrew's, dating back to about 1500, is a prominent landmark.

The school has all the modern cricket facilities you could wish for, including an ex-county professional Martin Speight (Sussex and Durham) as coach, who oversees an all-year-round coaching programme, a stylish pavilion and a digital scoreboard. According to the prospectus, 'Our indoor facilities are excellent with a new four-bay net system, 1,000 lux lighting, two bowling machines, video analysis room and software, while outside there are five grounds and a new six-bay artificial net system.' In the summer

eight sides are fielded for whom fixtures are arranged at the appropriate level.

The culmination of the 1st XI season is the BOWS Festival in which the school competes alongside Brighton College, Oakham, and Wellington College, in a competition that Sedbergh has regularly won. The school also enters the 1st XI National Twenty20 which they won in 2017, beating Millfied, while the U15s have won the National Twenty20 competition once and twice been runners-up.

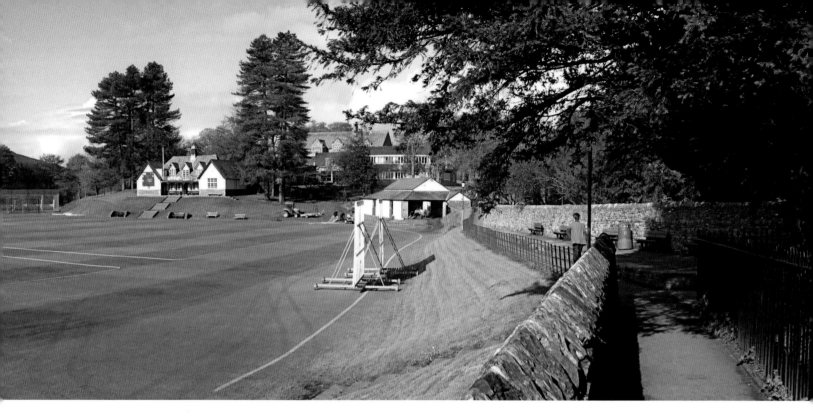

Four of Sedbergh's Old Boys are recent cricket professionals: Harry Brook and George Hill (both Yorkshire), Jordan Clark with Lancashire and Jamie Harrison at Durham. Clark achieved the ultimate batting achievement of hitting six sixes in an over in a 2nd XI game against Yorkshire in 2013, the first English professional cricketer to do so.

The school hosts Minor Counties cricket on occasion, including Cumberland v. Lincolnshire in 2015. In 2019, the ground hosted the first-ever first-class game in Cumbria as a home game for Lancashire when Lancashire, including Jimmy Anderson, played Durham.

Home to: Sedbergh School Cricket Team

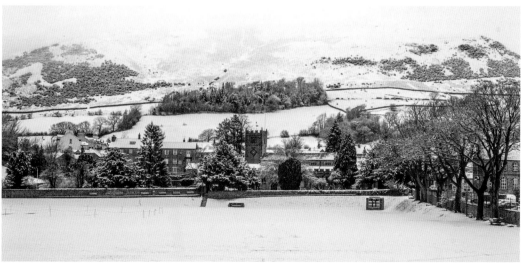

Newlands Cricket Ground

Cape Town, South Africa

When cricket first arrived at Newlands, this part of the Western Cape was heavily wooded with pine trees. The nascent Western Province Cricket Club took out a 25-year lease on the site in 1888 for £100 per annum. Each life member of the club was expected to donate £25 towards the costs of acquiring the ground and £350 was raised for the cost of a suitable pavilion. The first fixture played was a two-day match between 'Mother Country' and 'Colonial Born'.

Only five years after Test cricket was played at Lord's, Newlands hosted its first Test match in 1889 between England and South Africa, which ended in a victory for the visiting side by an innings and 202 runs. South Africa scored 47 and 43 with nine of the batsmen bowled out in the second innings.

The match may not have been memorable, but the location made a deep impression on England's winning captain Aubrey Smith:

'Newlands Cricket Ground was a picture to be remembered, with its surrounding mass of pines, overtopped by the great Table Mountain, on one side the new stand covered with red cloth standing out prominently against the green background. The picturesque effect given on our own grounds being enhanced by the bright and varied colour of many Malay women in their holiday attire.'

South Africa finally turned the tables on England in the second of two Test matches played at Newlands in 1906, with another win in 1910. It would be another 60 years before the next victory at Newlands in 1970, against the Australians under Bill Lawry.

In 1902 attendance records were broken as 10,000 cricket fans crowded into the ground to watch the first visit of the Australians. Between 1991 and 1997 numerous changes were made to the ground. Large portions of the grass embankments were replaced by pavilions, increasing the seating capacity to 25,000. The capacity of the stadium makes it worthy of Test-venue status, but it is the unparalleled setting that stands it apart.

As Newlands is used for cricket only about 35 days a year, extra income will be generated through the sale of stadium naming rights to Six Gun Grill and a major commercial redevelopment of the precinct. The first phase will be completed in July 2021 and the second in 2022. Rugby will no longer be played here: from 2021, the Stormers and Western Province will be moving to Cape Town.

Home to: The Cape Cobras

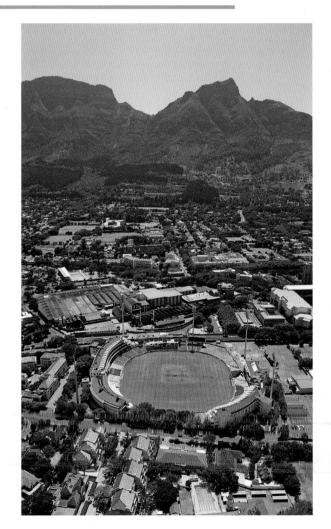

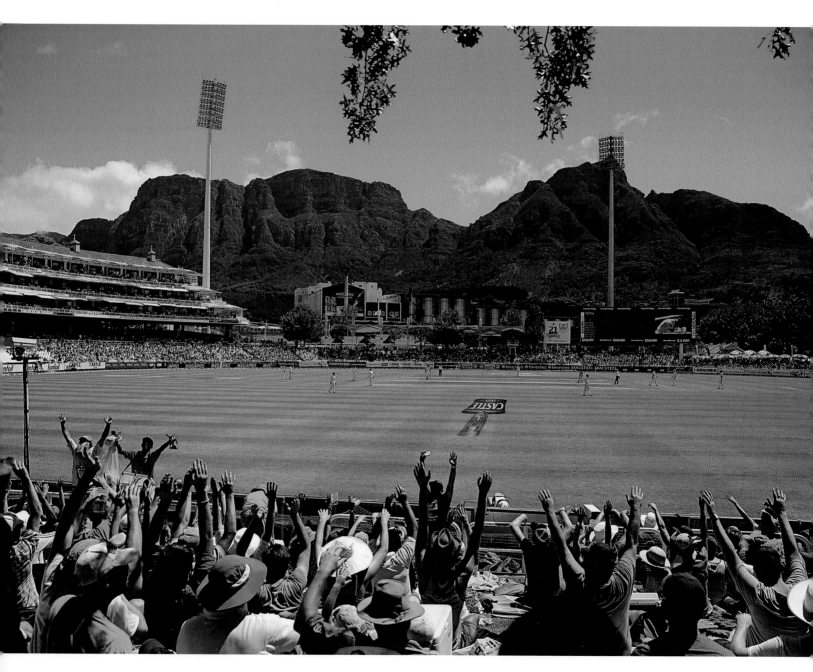

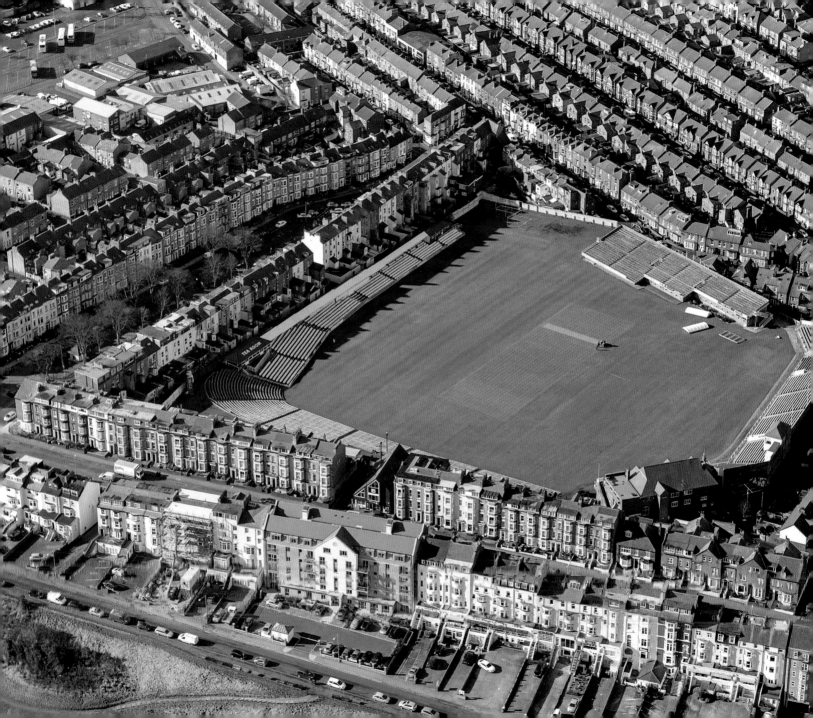

North Marine Road Ground

Scarborough, North Yorkshire, England

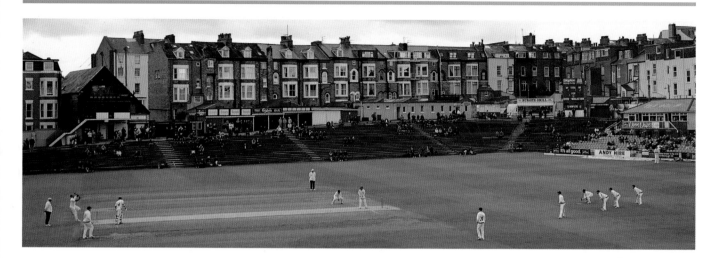

Scarborough Cricket Club, formed in 1849, moved from Castle Hill to North Marine Road in 1863 and has stayed there ever since. North Marine Road has hosted Yorkshire League fixtures, County Championship matches, one-day games and, of course, the magnificent Scarborough Cricket Festival, which began in 1876 and has been held annually except for the years during the two World Wars.

Scarborough is heaving with incomers at the end of August and beginning of September. Cricket fans can see star players while holidaymakers enjoy the sun, sea, rest, chip shops and amusement arcades. When Alan Lee of *The Times* visited in 2002 he rated the North Marine Road ground and its facilities higher than Test grounds such as Edgbaston, Old Trafford, the Oval and Headingley.

The 1876 cricket festival eventually settled into a format of three three-day matches, which brought the world's best players to Scarborough. In 1878 the club bought the land in North Marine Road, the ground was levelled and facilities improved. The current pavilion was built in 1896 and the North Stand erected in 1926. Crowds were huge in the late 1940s and a match against Derbyshire was attended by 22,946 people.

Festival cricket has provided spectators with cavalier entertainment. In 1875 C.I. Thornton scored 107 in just over an hour, including one six which saw the ball hit a chimney on a nearby house. In 1885 W.G. Grace scored 174 out of 263 for Gentlemen v. Players, a fixture that continued until 1962, when the distinction between amateur gentlemen and professional players was abolished.

According to Jon Griffin of the *Birmingham Post*, North Marine Road still retains a flavour of that era. In 2013 he wrote that 'Scarborough Cricket Ground could come straight out of a Lowry painting. It's as timeless as walking into the Cheshire Cheese in Fleet Street, where (both) Dr Johnson and Dickens drank.' Perhaps that is part of its charm, for both players and spectators.

It is the last of Yorkshire's out-grounds of which it once had many. Well described by former *Northern Echo* news editor Mike Amos: 'Now only Scarborough survives, a sort of not-out out-ground.'

Home to: Scarborough Cricket Club;

Oval Maidan

Mumbai, India

Maidan means park or open space in Urdu and big cities like Mumbai have a good number of them, many very sizeable. The Azad Maidan, where a 14-year-old Sachin Tendulkar once shared a then world-record batting partnership of 664 with Vinod Kambli, measures 25 acres.

A couple of miles away is the Oval Maidan, a Grade I recreational area, lying within a circumference of coconut palms and described as 'one of Mumbai's prettiest open spaces'. It currently measures 22 acres but is likely to lose a bit of that in the next two or three years. Think how many games can be going on in a space like that on a Sunday in cricket-mad India. The playing area is permanent home to six of the larger south Mumbai clubs, who each rent an area of the ground. Local schools and corporate cricket teams book on an occasional basis and organise Twenty20 competitions. However, the ground has a lot of extra space so it is relatively easy to hire a pitch for about 2,000 rupees (about £20), relatively costly in Indian terms. Ground care is organised partly by the clubs and partly by the Oval Maidan.

The area is an architectural treasure trove. On one side of the park the street is lined with neo-Gothic structures, including the Venetian Gothic-style University Building, the High Court and the Rajabai Clock Tower, which houses the university library and is modelled

on the Elizabeth Tower (Big Ben). These buildings once formed the waterfront, as the maidan was established on part of a large tract of land reclaimed from the Arabian Sea in the 1920s. Seventeen stunning Art Deco buildings were also constructed on the new land, forming the other side of the park. Because of the unique juxtaposition of these very different architectural styles, there was pressure for the Oval Maidan and the area around it to be recognised as a World Heritage Site. This was granted in 2018.

When Pope Paul VI became the first pontiff to visit India in 1964, he celebrated mass in the maidan, which was renamed in his honour. But by the 1990s the ground, owned and run by the state government, had become very run down and 'frequented by beggars, prostitutes and drug peddlers', according to one long-time resident. During the monsoon 'the grass would grow as high as five feet but the authorities weren't bothered about mowing it'. Eventually the residents, with help from local businesses, won a court case and £150,000 was raised to restore the maidan. 'We installed a mile long, high-quality steel fence at the ground's circumference', says Mrs Pooja Patel. 'We had invited the then Governor of Maharashtra, the late Dr. P.C. Alexander, to inaugurate the newly restored Oval Maidan; he was really happy that the Trust had changed the face of the ground.'

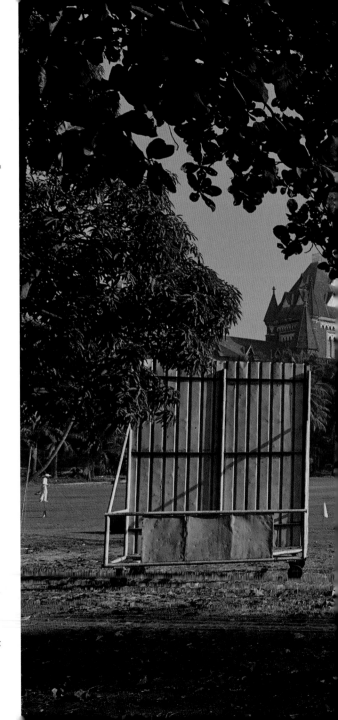

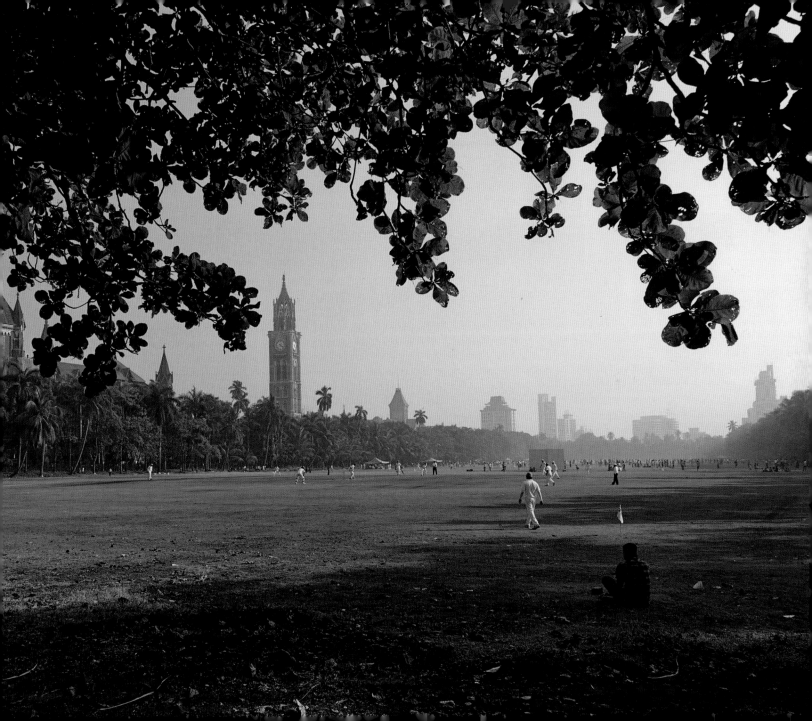

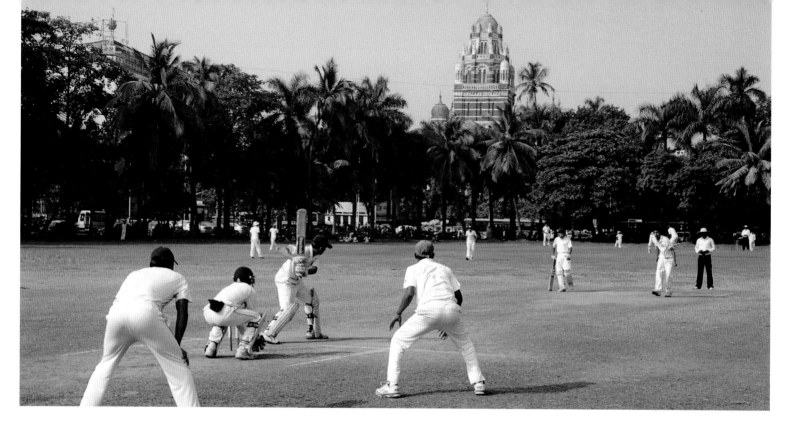

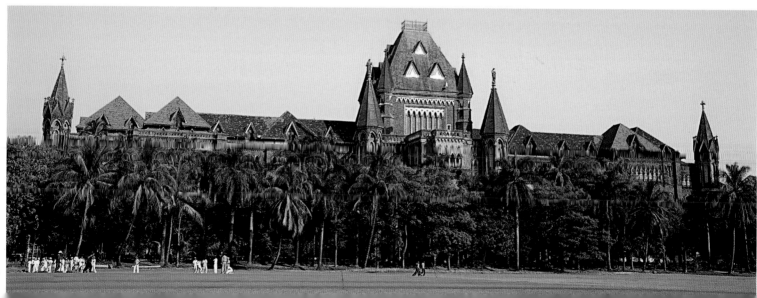

From the volume of cricket taking place, the Mumbai maidan seems like a vibrant and attractive arena for young players to learn the ropes. But according to Shishir Hattangadi, an ex-player and former Mumbai selector, it is some years since Mumbai was a force in national cricket. Twenty years or so have passed since players of the calibre of Tendulkar, Gavaskar and Shastri emerged from this kind of environment. Hattangadi thinks the new generation is developing in smaller centres, because facilities are now available across the country, perhaps not such a bad thing. But a new factor, the razzmatazz and glamour of the IPL, may yet swing the focus back to the big cities.

In the meantime, supporters of the Oval Maidan are facing a new battle. The government has announced plans for India's first underground Metro line in Mumbai, the route of which will impact on both the Azad and Oval maidans. Roughly 3,995 square metres (43,000 square feet) of the Oval Maidan is earmarked, but the Mumbai Metro Rail Corporation has promised that none of the cricket pitches will be touched, although 'some trees' will have to go. The disruption is envisaged to last about five years.

Home to: Six teams, including Elf Vengsarkar Cricket Academy and Elphinstone College Gymkhana

LEFT: The Bombay High Court (above) and the Western Railway Headquarters (below) form a dramatic backdrop to the Oval Maidan.

BELOW: The University of Mumbai's Rajabai Clock Tower is another of the Oval Maidan's surrounding landmarks. It was designed by Sir George Gilbert Scott and is based on London's Elizabeth Tower (Big Ben).

BELOW: The cricket ground is framed by a variety of architecturally significant buildings, including the Art Deco-style Eros Cinema shown here.

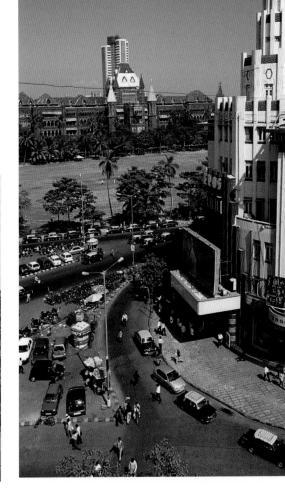

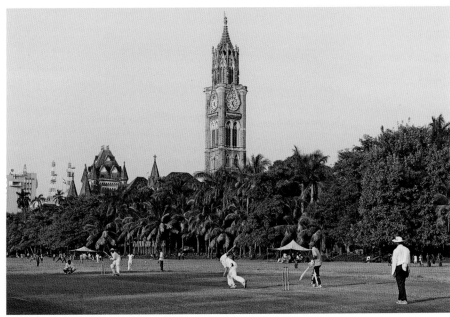

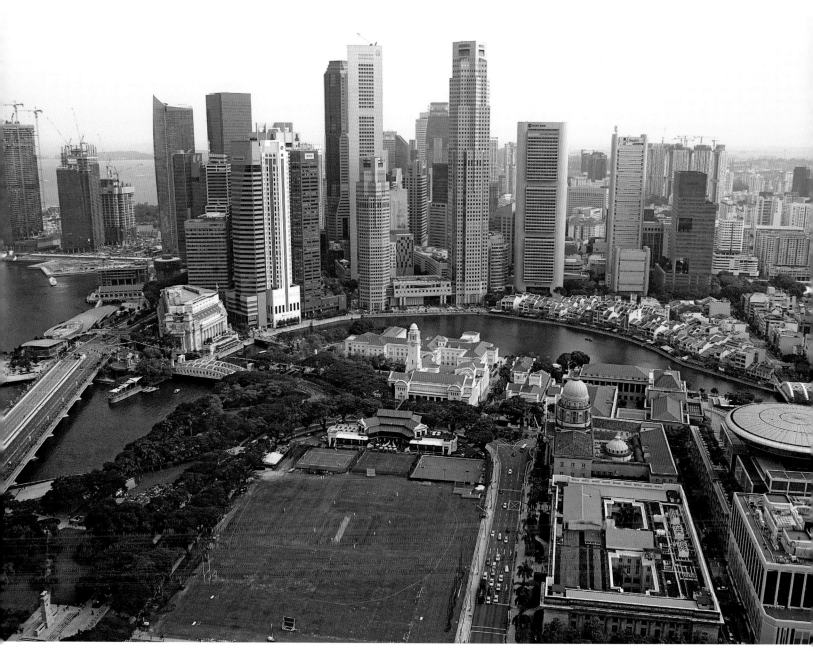

Padang Field

Singapore

The Padang Field in Singapore is remarkable, not only for its backdrop of soaring high-rises in the neighbouring business district, but for the price the land it occupies would command if ever it were turned over for commercial development.

Cricket has a long history in Singapore, dating back to 1837, and the Padang (the Malay for 'field') is one of the main venues. Close to City Hall, St Andrew's Cathedral and the Old Supreme Court, and overlooked by towering skyscrapers, it is an exciting and vibrant venue. One end of the ground, which has hosted neutral ODIs, is officially called the Supreme Court and Parliament House End, which must be a bit of a mouthful in commentary.

Two teams play here. As each has its own cricket area and pavilion at opposite ends of the ground, it is more stadium-sharing than ground-sharing. Relations between the two organisations have been described as 'friendly yet competitive'. The test would be what happens if the ball from one game encroaches on the other's playing area.

The Singapore Cricket Club occupies the southern end and organised the first cricket played in Singapore, although the club itself was not founded till 1852. The club had early tries at building pavilions in the 1860s and 1877, but it is the third development in 1884 that forms the basis for today's pavilion. At the other end, the Singapore Recreation Club, which began as the Straits Cricket Club

in 1881, also offers sports, such as tennis, hockey and rugby.

Although the national side has yet to take part in the World Cup, the standard of cricket in Singapore continues to improve, underpinned by a great increase in player numbers. In 2019 Padang Field was officially listed as a National Monument.

Home to: Singapore Cricket Club; Singapore Recreation Club

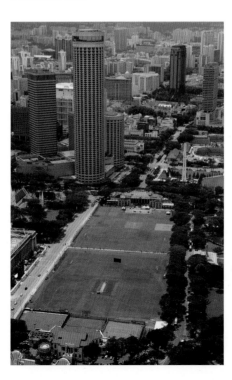

BELOW LEFT: The red-roofed pavilion in the foreground belongs to Singapore Cricket Club (the Supreme Court and Parliament House End); the pavilion at the opposite (north) end of the Padang belongs to Singapore Recreation Club.

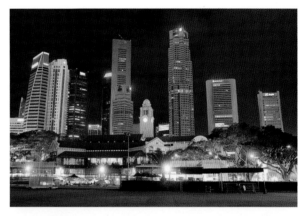

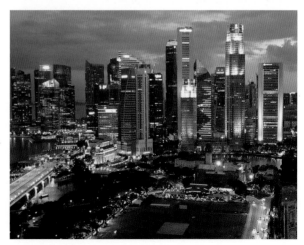

The Parks

Oxford, England

Not far from Oxford's city centre is a large tranquil area called the Parks. It is very spacious, about 70 acres, and was designed as an arboretum and for recreational purposes. Cricket has been played here since 1881 but the playing area is only about 3 acres and you may have to ask for directions. The bushes, trees and plants make it a very pleasant walk and you might well be following in the footsteps of Charles II who is thought to have walked his dog here, a spaniel, no doubt.

The main landmark to look for is the pavilion. It dates back to 1881 and was designed by Sir Thomas Jackson, the architect of many Oxford University buildings. Jackson, or perhaps someone else, had the happy idea of siting it the same distance from the wicket as the Lord's pavilion. Other than that, only the sight screens, a rope marking the boundary, a couple of nearby nets and a few wooden benches mark out that this is a first-class cricket ground.

In April, before the season proper begins, first-class counties play here for a little light warm-up. The batsmen build their confidence with a high score and the bowlers get some easy wickets. Against a youthful, inexperienced university side, a draw is a bad result for the county team. The professionals use these matches to flex their muscles and sometimes achieve extraordinary figures. In April 2005 the New Zealand Test player Craig Spearman, playing for Gloucestershire, hit an over from Luke Moreton, a leg-spinner playing for Oxford UCCE, for five sixes and a four, a total of 34. It was the unfortunate Moreton's first over in first-class cricket.

Normally these games are sparsely attended, but in April 2015 word spread that Kevin Pietersen, in bad odour with the England selectors, was playing for Surrey against MCC Universities Oxford as he attempted a comeback to the England team. The crowd was three deep to see him score a typically destructive 170. And all for free – the Parks is the only first-class venue in England which does not charge for admission, though your appreciation of the day's cricket in the form of a small donation is always welcomed by the volunteer collectors.

But usually the cricket is lower key and at the end of the day you can continue your stroll round the Parks and head out via the duck pond and the River Cherwell, which winds its way along one side of the park.

Home to: Oxford University Cricket Club

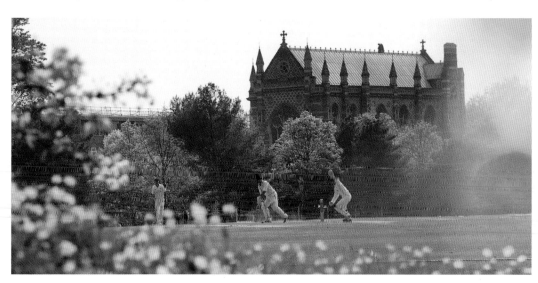

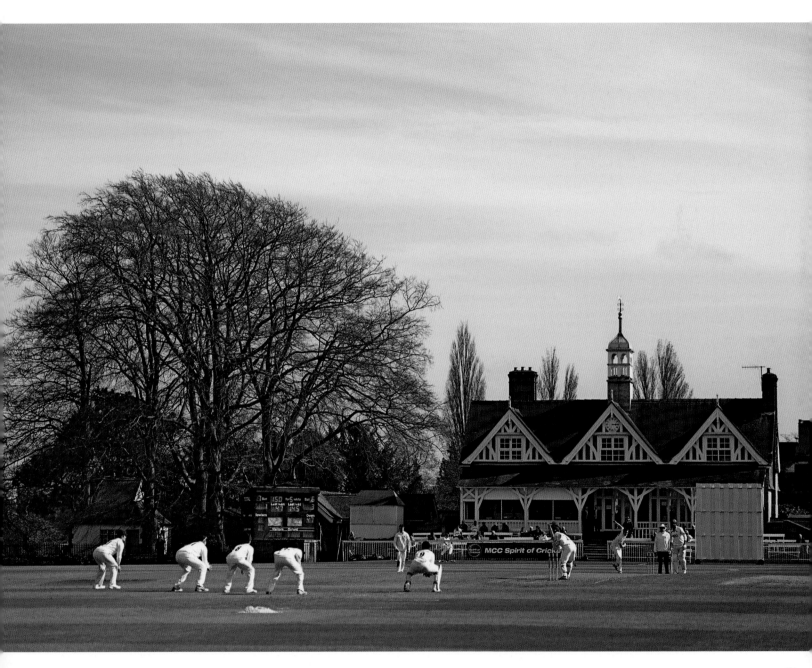

Pukekura Park

New Plymouth, North Island, New Zealand

Playing and watching cricket at Pukekura Park must demand a lot of concentration because there is so much all around that is beautiful and distracting. The park is one of the four cricket homes of the Central District Stags, one of New Zealand's six first-class teams that contest the Plunket Shield.

Distinguished New Zealand Test players like Bev Congdon, Martin Crowe, Ian Smith and Ross Taylor have played in this temperate climate which, as well as encouraging the growth of all kinds of exotic flowers, plants and trees, also aids late swing. Lakes, boating and summertime concerts complete an idyllic scene. Founded in 1876, the park was originally a barren and swampy valley. Somewhere in its grounds is a 2,000-year-old Puriri tree and there are Japanese and Chinese gardens. More prosaically, the construction of a bridge named the Poet's Bridge was not a lyrical inspiration but paid for from the winnings on a horse called The Poet. With all these features and more, it is no surprise that the New Zealand Trust gives the park a five-star rating.

Cricket was first played here in 1892. The design of the grassed spectator terraces seems to be inspired by pyramids or ziggurats although they are apparently natural; if the Aztecs had played cricket, this is how they would have built their grounds. *Wisden* has described Pukekura Park as one of the six best grounds in the world to watch cricket.

One ODI has been played here, Sri Lanka v. Zimbabwe in 1992, but the ground missed out on hosting the 2015 World Cup games. The management wasn't surprised, acknowledging that the infrastructure demanded by the ICC wasn't in place. But they made sure of hosting three of the qualifying matches by spending $194,000 donated by the Community Trust on improving the cricket training nets. With so many beautiful grounds in New Zealand, the tournament organisers can afford to be ultra-choosy. But if scenic glory were the only criterion, it is hard to see how Pukekura Park could be rejected.

Home to: Central District Stags Cricket Club

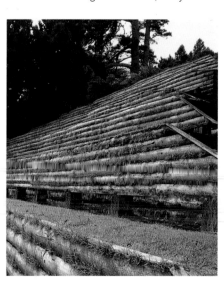

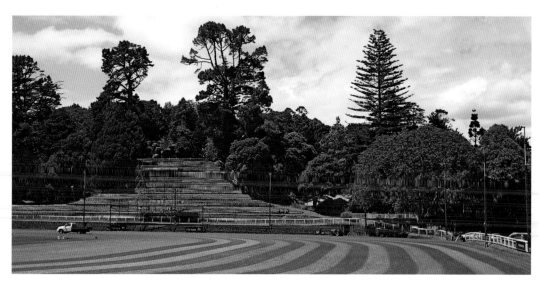

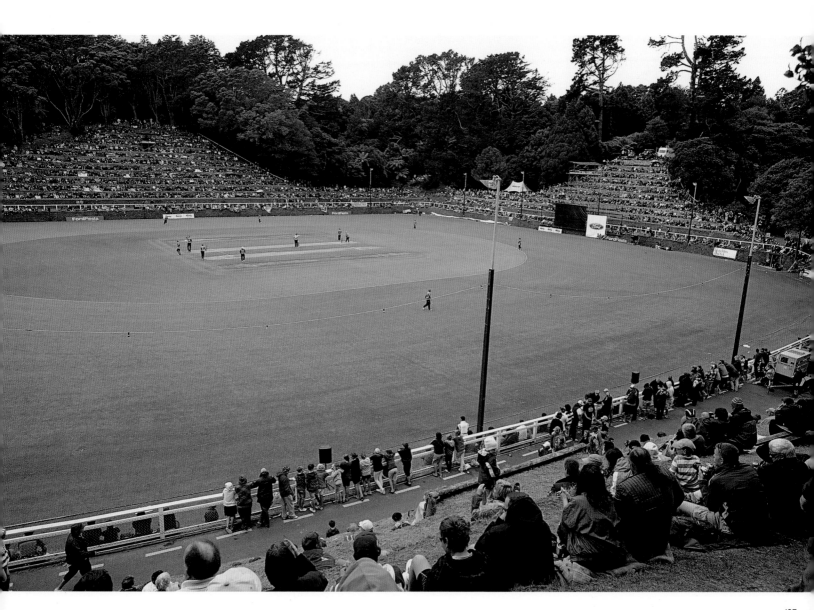

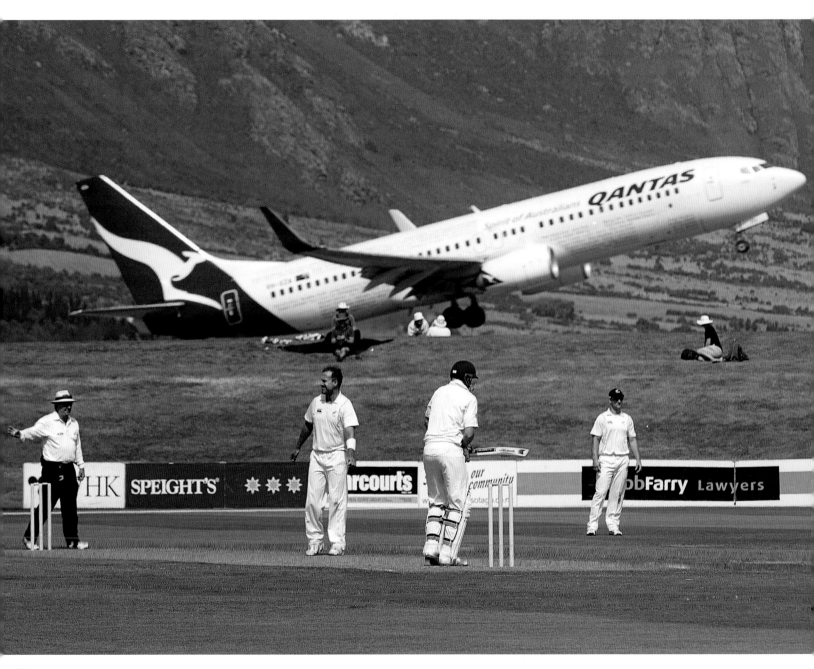

Queenstown Events Centre

Queenstown, South Island, New Zealand

If beauty of location was the qualification for selecting a Test ground, then the prosaically named Queenstown Events Centre would be a regular New Zealand Test venue. Its backdrop is one of the most sublime of any cricket ground. Bordering the shores of the picturesque Lake Wakatipu, behind it rises a spectacular mountain range called the Remarkables, aptly so in the case of this book. The area was used as a film location for many scenes from *The Lord of the Rings*, as was the nearby Fiordland National Park. With bungee jumping, trekking and mountaineering on offer, the Queenstown area has been called 'the adventure capital of the world'. It has also earned a reputation as a party town and hit the headlines when members of the England rugby team allegedly misbehaved in a club during the 2011 Rugby World Cup.

If there is a fly in the ointment for cricket lovers, perhaps it is the nearby Queenstown international airport. Planes fly so low over the ground that they seem to have taken off in the outfield and the umpire appears to be signalling to the pilot not to fly behind the bowler's arm. With up to 12 departures an hour, it is potentially very disruptive. Or, if you're a plane-spotting cricket lover, heaven.

Opened in 1997, Queenstown is one of the most southerly first-class grounds in the world, although not quite so far south as Dunedin. It can seat 6,000 with extra temporary seating of 13,000. Although the ground has hosted ODIs, it has never found favour with the administrators who select Test venues. It was not even one of the seven New Zealand sites selected for the 2015 World Cup. However, it is very well used by Queenstown CC, the local club, which has excellent facilities including four turf wickets, two artificial wickets and both indoor and outdoor practice facilities. The club fields two

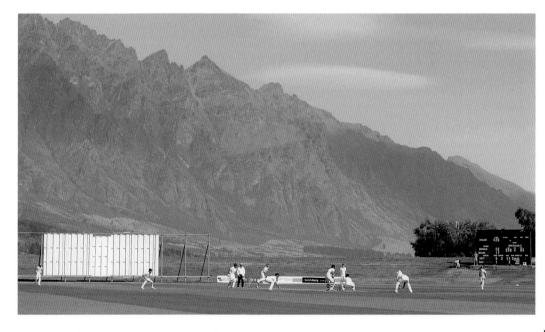

teams in the senior grade competition and has a thriving junior section.

Perhaps Queenstown's population of 13,000 is judged too small for Tests, or its facilities are not up to par – although it *did* host the West Indies touring team in 2020. Whatever the case, locals can console themselves that even if the ground doesn't make the shortlist for Tests, it is often in the top 10 of most people's lists of beautiful grounds. Maybe a change of name would improve its chances, as recommended by the Australian sports journalist Will Macpherson. He suggested it could be renamed the Remarkables Cricket Ground, after the nearby mountain range, because, as he says, 'it is just that'.

Home to: Queenstown Cricket Club

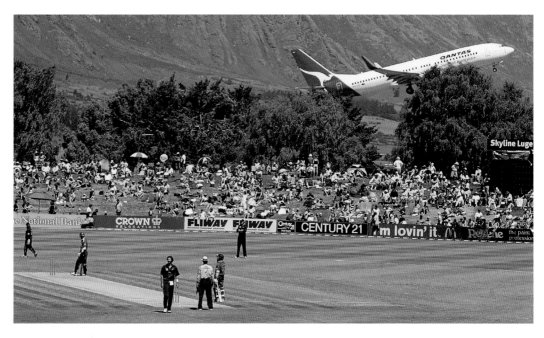

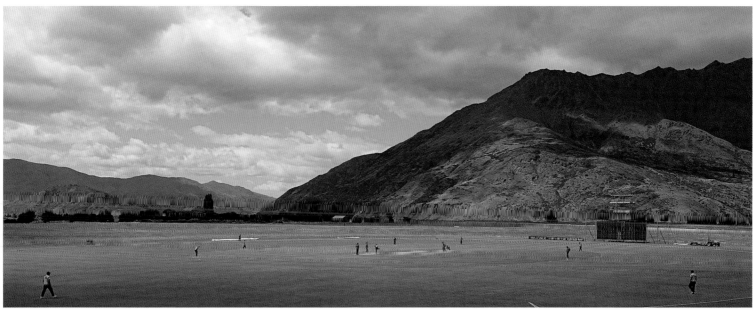

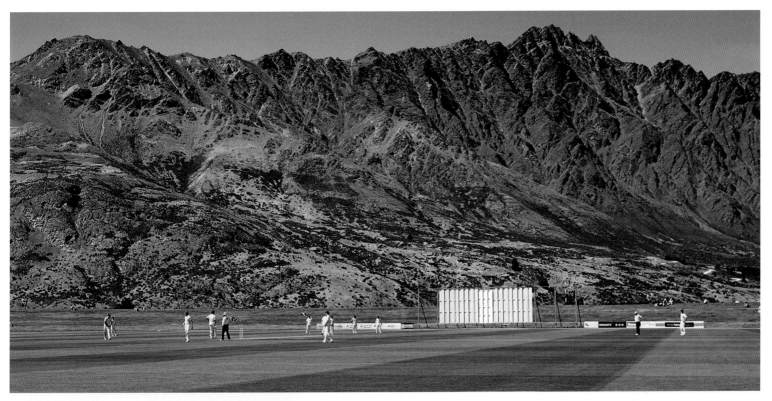

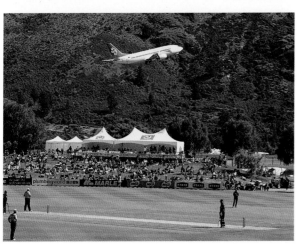

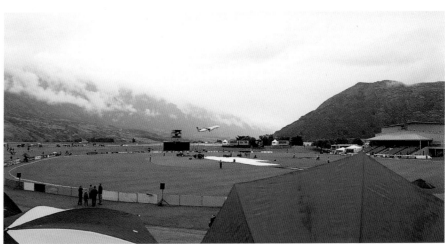

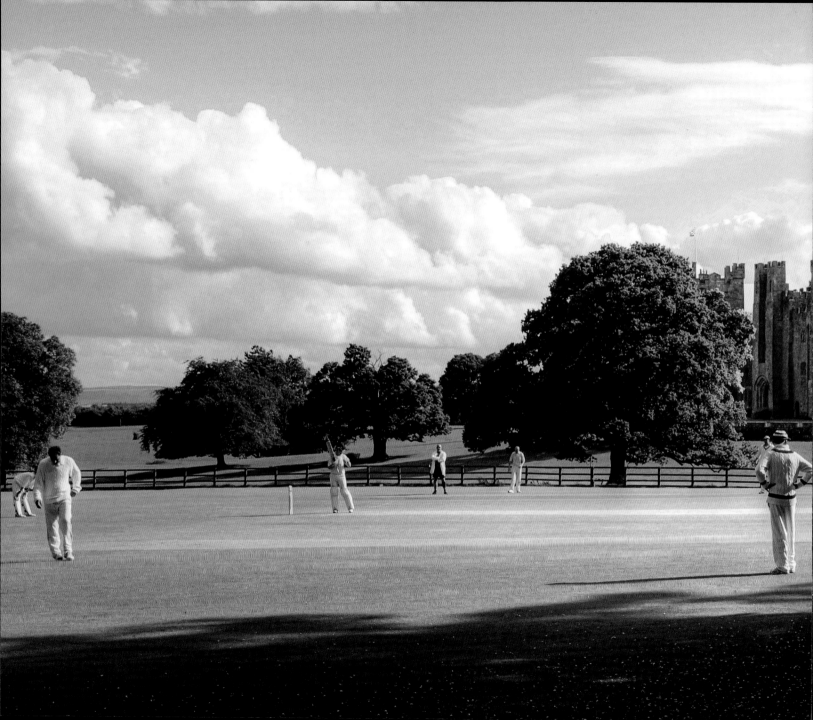

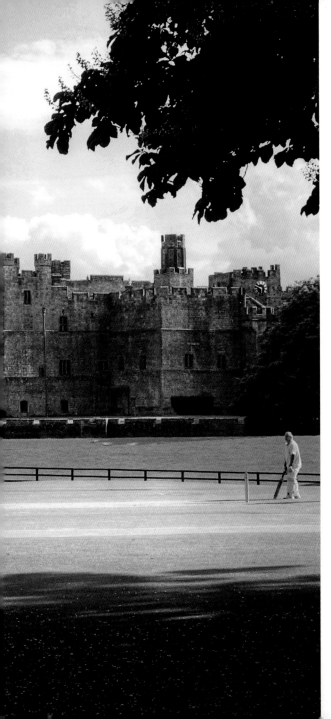

Raby Castle

Staindrop, County Durham, England

Raby Castle, which dates back to the 14th century, was built by the Neville family. Cecily Neville, mother of two English kings, Edward IV and Richard III, was born here in 1415. The family of the current owner, Henry Francis Cecil, 12th Baron Barnard, bought the castle in 1626 and it contains many fine paintings by Sir Peter Lely, Sir Anthony van Dyck, Sir Joshua Reynolds and Sir Alfred Munnings, among others.

The castle's associations with cricket go back a long way. It was the site of the first officially recorded game of cricket played in Durham in 1751 between the Earl of Northumberland's XI and the Duke of Cleveland's XI, an ancestor of the present owner. A match to commemorate the event was played in 1992 featuring the full Durham XI which included Lord I. T. Botham.

Raby Castle Cricket Club have played here since 1890 and enjoy excellent relations with their landlords. In 2015, the club celebrated its 125th Anniversary with an event in the entrance hall of the castle by kind permission of Lord Barnard, the club's patron. When a foot-and-mouth epidemic broke out in 1991, preventing the club from using the ground for the complete season, the castle very helpfully tended the square with a rotary lawn mower to keep it clear of thistles.

Strong links exist between the club and the county side and players from the club such as Neil Riddell and Ben Usher have gone on to play for Durham at various levels. The club plays in Division A of Darlington and District Cricket League and in 2015 won the Division A Knock-Out Cup.

Unlike some other grounds, hitting a tree at Raby Castle is not an automatic four and batsmen have to keep on running, unless the ball crosses the boundary, in which case it's four or six depending on whether it bounced. This begs the question, what would happen if the ball got lodged in the upper branches and took five minutes to retrieve? You can't be caught off a rebound, though. The wicket faces East/West and, following the loss of some trees, play is occasionally suspended because of the sun, or bowling takes place from one end only.

At one stage, the club used to change in an upstairs room in the castle above the coffee shop. It now has a basic but serviceable pavilion designed by the estate architect in the style of the castle's entry booth. However during Covid restrictions in 2020, the players had to arrive changed ready to play and bring their own tea. These measures were to avoid mixing in the pavilion and on top of that the fielding side had to sanitise their hands every six overs. These were ECB-specified rules and all clubs had to comply.

Home to: Raby Castle Cricket Club

The Ship Inn

Elie, Fife, Scotland

The idea of playing regular organised club cricket on a beach may seem improbable. But it is well known that cricket lovers look at any large unbuilt area as a challenge to organise a game. Normally it's on grass, but why exclude such a tempting space as the magnificent expanse of sand in front of the Ship Inn, Elie? And cricket has been played in some very unusual places, such as 5,180 metres (17,000 feet) up Mount Everest; the Brambles – a sandbank near the Isle of Wight, which periodically surfaces long enough to organise a game; and in 1823, by Captain William Parry's expedition on the island of Igloolik, at latitude three degrees north of the Arctic circle. But, unlike the Ship Inn's, these were occasional games.

Elie is in northeast Scotland on the north coast of the Firth of Forth, not far from where it becomes the North Sea. The pub dates back to 1838 and cricket has been played here since 1990. There are about 10 matches a year, including a cricket festival in August, and the MCC and the Edinburgh side, Grange CC, are regular visitors.

The special local conditions demand unusual ground rules. The ball is plastic because a hard one would not bounce. With little danger to one's shins, pads are not needed. The pitch gets a pre-match roll but the outfield remains as the tide left it. Kelp found on the square is removed and made into a boundary rope. The boundary is movable according to the state of the tide and local knowledge says it's better to bat second

when the tide has turned, because the boundary gets smaller. Interval refreshments come straight from the pub's menu, much of it locally caught. A pleasant ground rule entitles anyone hitting a six into the beer garden to their height in beer, achieved by the West Indian cricketer Richie Richardson among others.

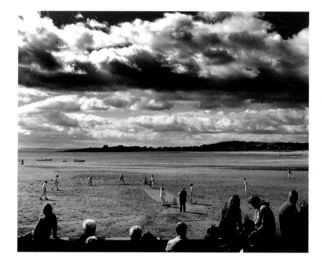

Cricket here is played with the degree of amused competitiveness that gives club cricket its own special charm. By the way, if someone starts talking about a 'fifer', check whether he has just taken five wickets or is simply from this part of the country.

Home to: The Ship Inn Cricket Club

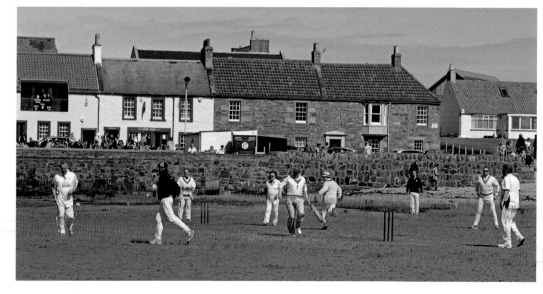

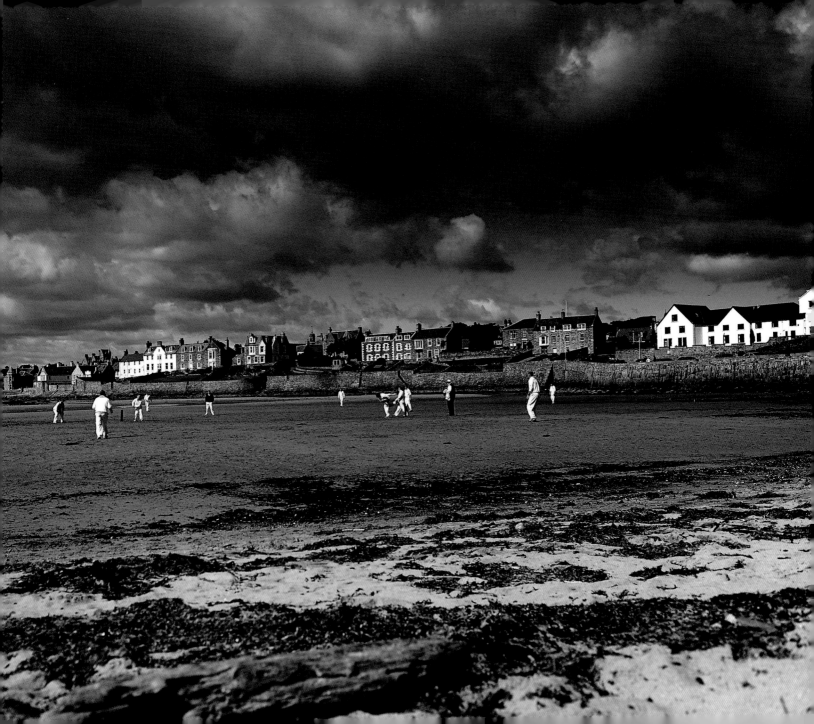

Sir Paul Getty's Ground

Wormsley Park, Buckinghamshire, England

This beautiful, quintessentially English ground in the heart of the Chiltern countryside was built by the American-born Sir Paul Getty. Getty was the elder son of the fourth marriage of John Paul Getty, perhaps the richest American of his era, and inherited much of his father's huge fortune.

Some time in the 1970s when he was suffering from depression, Getty was introduced to cricket by one of his neighbours, Sir Mick Jagger. While in hospital, he also met Sir Gubby Allen, an England cricket captain of the 1930s and 40s. Through these contacts, Getty gradually fell in love with the game and what he perceived as its traditional British values.

Struggling against heroin and alcohol addictions, Getty used cricket as therapy. When it worked, over the years he showed his gratitude in many ways. On moving to his new 3,000-acre estate at Wormsley, he decided it should have a cricket ground. He later said 'I took on more than I'd realised when I decided to have cricket there.' Harry Brind, the Surrey groundsman, and Brian Johnston, the BBC cricket commentator, were advisers, and the weather vane is modelled on 'Jonners' unmistakable profile.

What emerged was a perfect oval cricket ground with an immaculately thatched pavilion, complete with traditional red telephone box, backed by the Chiltern Hills. It opened in 1992 and the Queen Mother and the Prime Minister, Sir John Major,

were among the guests. Over the years, the ground has continued to welcome the great and the good to watch what are essentially celebrity games, although more competitive Minor Counties games also take place there. It is open to the public and you might like to round off a perfect day by attending a performance by Garsington Opera in the grounds of the estate.

Other Getty involvements with cricket included the purchase of *Wisden*, the cricket annual, and substantial donations towards the construction of the Mound Stand at Lord's. David Lloyd, when manager of England, presented Getty with an England cap and blazer as a thank-you. Getty also

bought what he thought was a complete collection of *Wisden* from Robert Maxwell, but it turned out to lack the first volume. Getty gave money to many iconic British institutions such as the National Gallery and St Paul's Cathedral. Eventually he took British citizenship and was knighted for services to philanthropy. Getty died in 2003, aged 70, and his widow took over the Wormsley estate, including the cricket ground. However, the will contained a direction that the estate and cricket ground should pass to Getty's second son Mark and his descendants after no more than seven years.

Home to: Sir Paul Getty XI

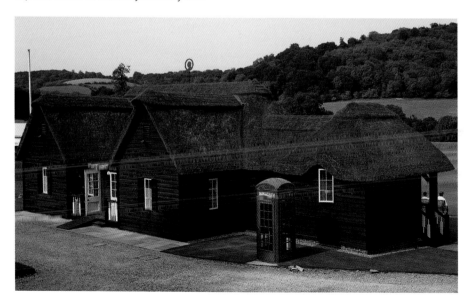

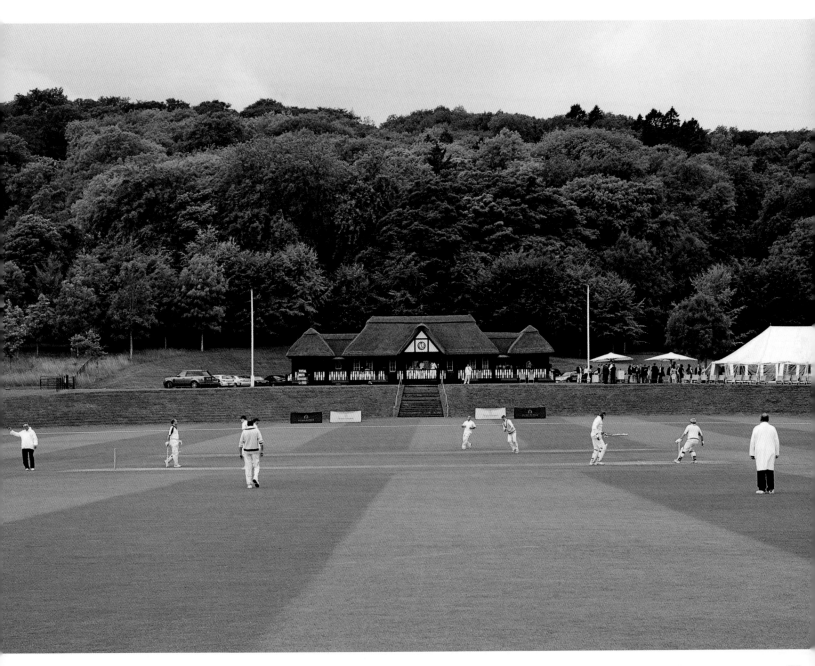

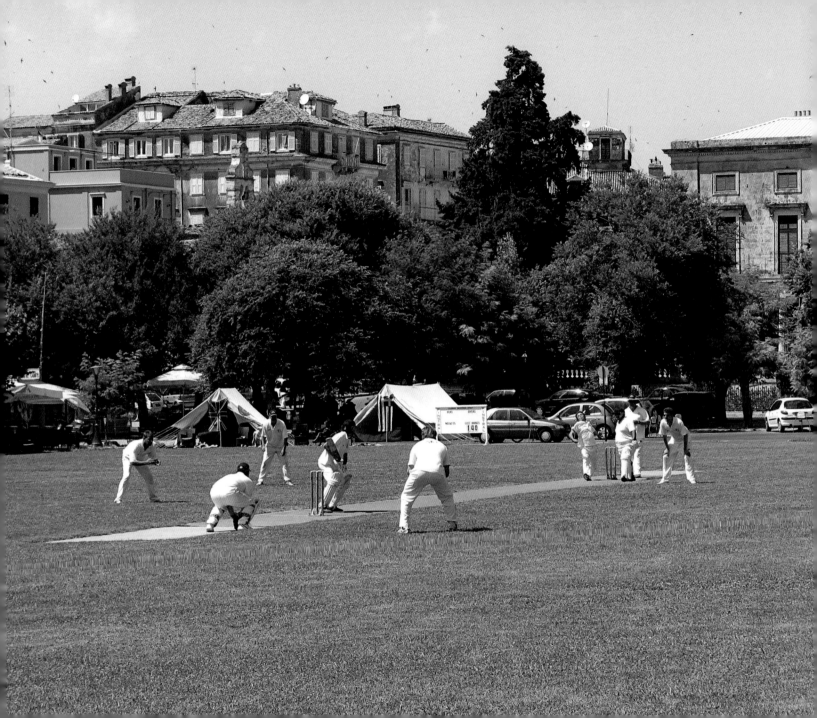

Spianada Square

Corfu, Greece

Cricket in Corfu has a long history dating back to 1823 when the first game to take place on the island was played between officers of the Royal Navy and the local British Garrison. The island was then a British protectorate and under this strong cricketing influence the Corfiots took to the game. For decades only two local sides existed, and after World War II cricket was at risk of dying out due to lack of funds and equipment. But in 1959 the British honorary consul on the island, Major John Forte, took the initiative by appealing for equipment. Fifty bats and 350 balls were donated by *Daily Telegraph* readers, which saved the day. The game has thrived since then with at least 20 clubs throughout Greece, most of them on Corfu.

With several cricket grounds, the island has a well-developed league system. Spianada Square, however, is the proverbial jewel in the crown. In the centre of Corfu's downtown district, with bustling shops and hotels all around, it provides an unusual cricketing environment. The nearby area, the Liston, is famous for its Italianate architecture and arched colonnade lined with cafés, tavernas and bars.

The island welcomes cricket tours and many British sides have played there. Teams enjoy a unique experience as Spianada Square is one of the few sports field anywhere within a UNESCO World Heritage Site. For good measure, it is the biggest square in Southeastern Europe and one of the largest in Europe. The ground, along with other

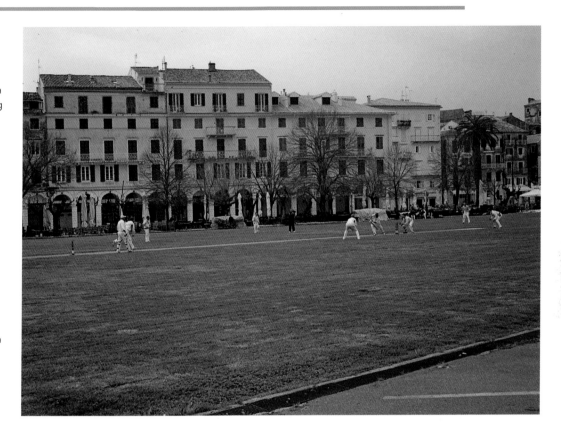

local grounds, has hosted European Cricket Council Trophy matches.

Greece has been a member of the International Cricket Council since 1995 and one of its interesting current initiatives is to encourage overseas players of Greek descent to develop the local cricket talent. As a result, the former Hampshire player Nic

Pothas began to take age-group teams from England to Corfu. He also provided coaching on his regular visits to the country, where many of his family still live. In 2012 Pothas captained the Greek national side at the European Twenty20 Championships Division 2 tournament, played in Corfu.

Home to: Twenty20 competitions

Spitfire Ground

St Lawrence, Canterbury, England

Cricket dotes on its curiosities. The famous 27-metre (90-foot) high lime tree at St Lawrence's Spitfire Ground, blown down in the storm of 2005, is a case in point. It was one of only three trees within the boundary of a ground where first-class cricket has been played, the others being the City Oval in Pietermaritzburg, South Africa and the VRA Cricket Ground in Amstelveen, the Netherlands.

The lime was already mature when Kent started playing at St Lawrence in 1847. Happily no one chopped it down, but it sometimes caused dispute if hit in the course of play. Eventually, the administrators came up with new rules especially for the tree. A batsman could not be out caught off the trunk, as reputedly once claimed. If struck by the ball, even on the full, the hit was worth four; the boundary and the tree had to be cleared to score a six, a carry of about 140 metres (460 feet).

In an obituary of the lime, Frank Keating of *The Guardian* wrote that only four batsmen achieved this. Three were among the big beasts of hitting: Learie Constantine of the West Indies (1928), Middlesex's Jim Smith (1939) and Carl Hooper of Kent (1992). The fourth was a little-known amateur, Arthur Watson of Sussex, in 1925.

Has the story of the lime overshadowed the long history of cricket on this ground? It depends how sentimental you are. On the one hand, the lime was already on borrowed time, having been diagnosed with fungus in 1999 and was expected to survive for only another 10 years. In anticipation of its demise, a successor had been selected and planted, though outside the playing area. Two months after the storm the new tree was relocated inside the playing area, although outside the boundary. It is hoped that over the years it will grow to the full majesty of its predecessor.

On the other hand, the ancient lime was the ground's pre-eminent landmark and witness to all the great feats of cricket on this ground and to all the great Kent names such as Alfred Mynn, Frank Woolley, A.P. 'Tich' Freeman, Les Ames, Colin Cowdrey, Alan Knott and Derek Underwood. Let Cowdrey have the last word:

'If I was given a choice as my last act on earth, it would be to walk to the wicket on the lovely St Lawrence Ground in the sunshine, with the pavilion chattering and the small tents buzzing. I would then lean into a half volley just outside off stump, praying that the old timing still lived in the wrists to send it speeding down the slope past cover's left hand to the old tree for four.'

Home to: Kent County Cricket Club

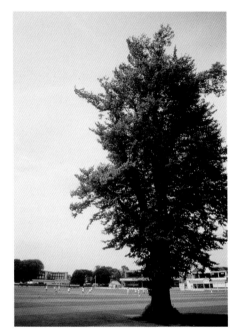

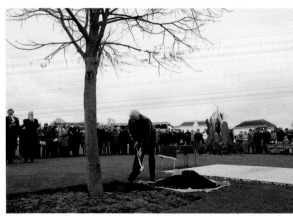

RIGHT: St Lawrence's famous lime tree (top) stood within the boundary of the ground until it was destroyed in the storm of 2005. In the photo below its replacement is being planted outside the boundary. The remains of its predecessor can be seen behind.

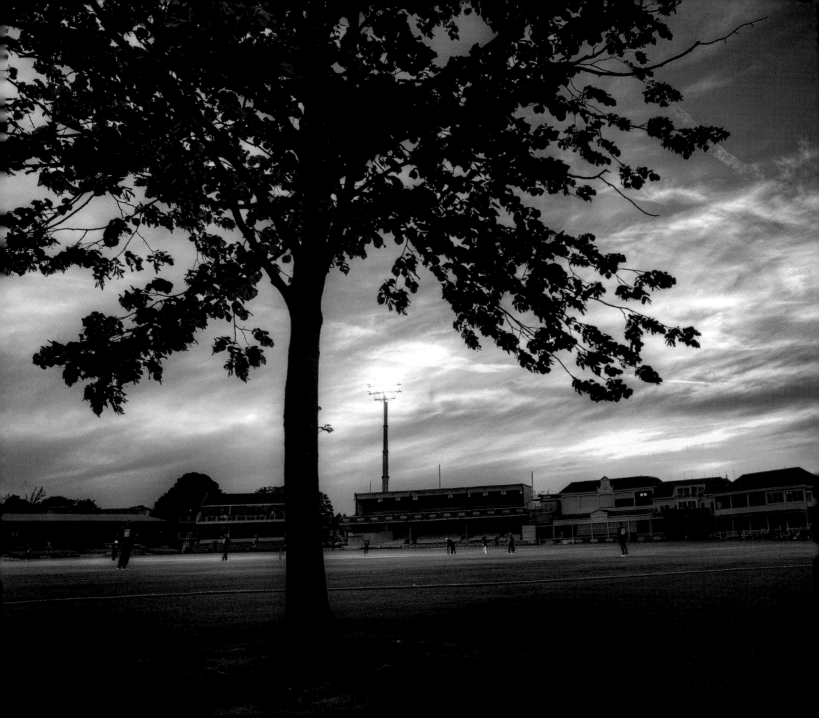

Spout House

Bilsdale, North Yorkshire, England

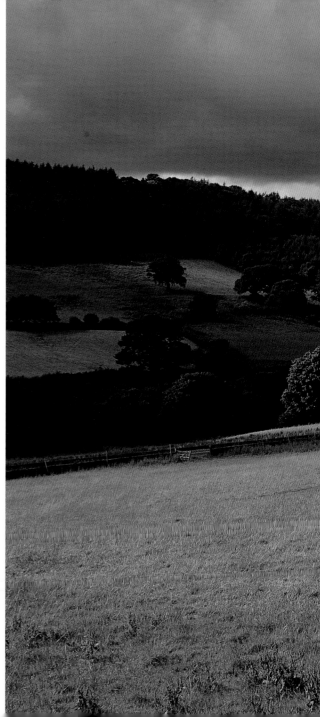

No one is quite sure when Spout House Cricket Club started, but old scorebooks and anecdotal evidence suggest the mid-19th century. Unarguably, from then till 2012 there were only three club secretaries. Numbers two and three were grandfather and grandson, William Ainsley, from 1874 to 1950, and William George Ainsley, from 1950 to 2012, making a barely believable span of 138 years for two members of the one family.

The Ainsleys made their living from sheep farming and still do. They also ran the Sun Inn at the bottom of the field until just prior to William George's death. On match days the ground is cleared of sheep, which are put into a neighbouring field, although at nearby Farndale they don't bother even to do that.

Creating a playing surface was a challenge: the grass can grow up to 15 centimetres (6 inches) high and the ground has a slope of one in seven. A small area was cleared three wickets wide to make the pitch, which is kept flattish by a Victorian sandstone roller, probably unique in current cricket. The grass outside the wicket is allowed to grow as it may and presents certain fielding problems. Visiting teams should check the

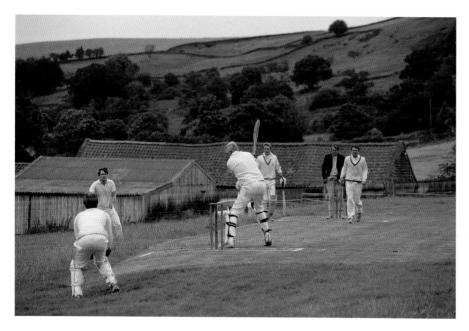

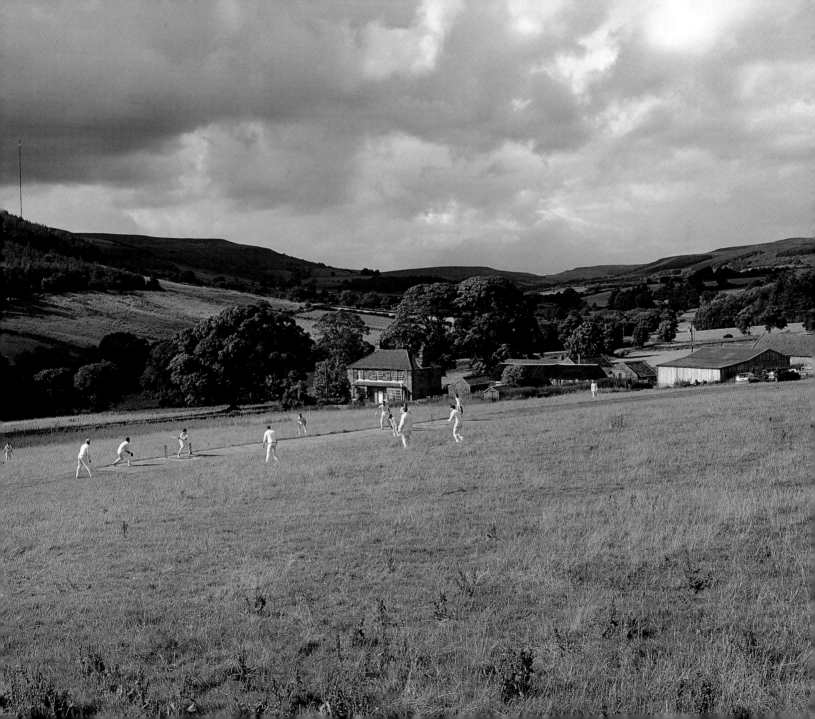

ground rules. To earn a six, you have to clear the stone wall perimeter; hitting it on the full only earns you four. In the outfield, the ball can frequently disappear into the thick grass and while fielders cluster round looking for it, batsmen are free to run as many as they can. Calling 'lost ball' at the sixth run usually ends the spree. Few fielders are strong enough to reach the wicket with a single uphill throw from the boundary, so away sides need to be alert with a relay system. Square leg umpires soon realise there is no point standing on the downward slope as the popping crease isn't visible. The field is entered through the farmyard where a hen hut and the stone roller all become on-field hazards. Midges are irritating, although not as bad as at Castleton where the bowler has

to use one hand to sweep them away in his delivery stride so he can see to the other end of the wicket.

Despite these obstacles, Spout House attracts a good class of visitor. Legend has it that W.G. Grace was once bowled for a golden duck by the blacksmith. Prince Ranjitsinhji, who had friends in the area, is also reputed to have played here, and Prince Harry, as house guest of the Countess of Mexborough, who lives nearby, has played at Spout House twice.

The original pavilion was a little wooden hut bought second-hand in the 1970s. It was rather basic with only one shared changing area and became known as 'the hen hut'.

When time came to replace it in 2009, you might have thought the club would have gone for an updated model. But they're traditional folk in these parts and they simply replaced it with as exact a replica of the original as they could.

Local cricket in the dales is less thriving than it used to be. Spout House plays in the Feversham League, which has only four teams. Unusually, the club is not centred on a local village so recruiting players is that much more difficult. Local farmers provide the nucleus of the team. Home games are played on Tuesday evenings from mid-May to June in a Twenty20 format, but it's all very flexible. Only the commitment of members has kept the club going up until now. They have done it partly for love of the game and partly in memory of William George, who wanted the club to continue. At the start of the first home game after his death, he was honoured with a minute's silence. Set in the top boundary wall, a memorial stone stands next to one commemorating his grandfather – a fitting tribute to their unparalleled records of service.

However the prospects for further games in the sheep meadow look bleak The club weren't able to raise 11 men throughout the 2019 season and relied on borrowing players from the opposition for games in the Feversham League. Coupled with a vertiginous pitch that is hard to maintain, Spout's future as one of the most scenic, extraordinary spots to play cricket is seriously in doubt.

Home to: Spout House Cricket Club

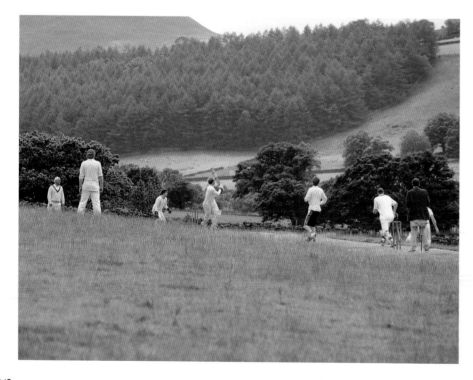

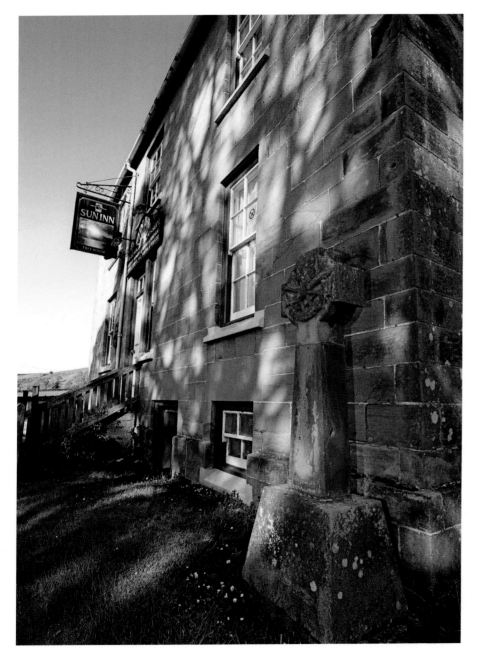

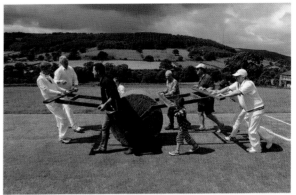

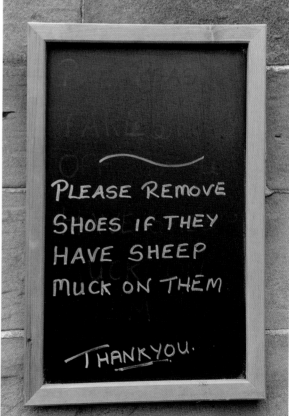

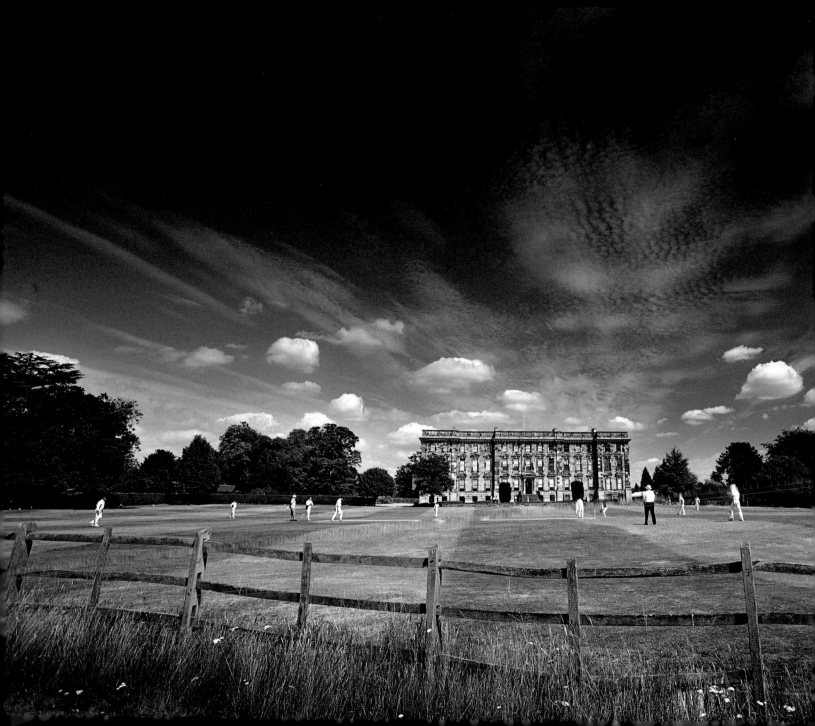

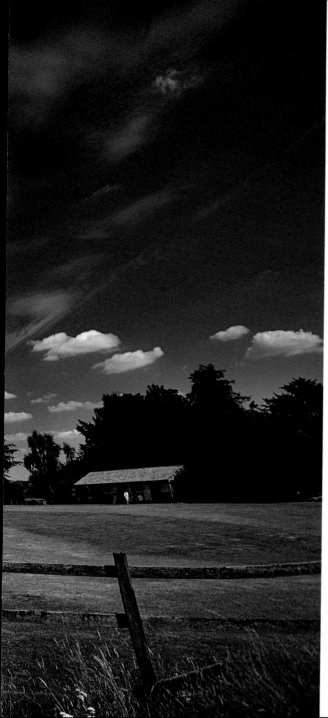

Stoneleigh Abbey

Warwickshire, England

Cricket has been played in this superb setting since 1839, when Sir Chandos Leigh laid out a ground for his son William to play on during the holidays from Harrow School. Stoneleigh Abbey was once a monastery dating back to the 12th century. It came into the possession of the Leigh family in the 16th century after the Dissolution of the Monasteries when it was converted into a large country house. The photograph is of the west wing, built around 1720.

It was William's younger brother Edward who went on to achieve cricketing prominence. He played in three winning Oxford University teams from 1852 to 1854, though he scored a total of only eight runs in all the matches and may well have owed his place to his specialist fielding at long-stop.

The first significant match on the ground took place in 1849 when the club played Rugby School. Edward's last game was in 1872, aged 40, when Fourteen Gentlemen of Warwickshire played a two-day game against the well-known travelling side I Zingari. His playing days over, he continued to involve himself in cricket and became President of the MCC in 1887.

Stoneleigh Abbey is now converted into flats and owned by a trust. The noblesse oblige connection has also disappeared, which,

more than 100 years ago, rewarded one of the Stoneleigh batsmen with a sixpence from Lord Leigh for hitting a six through one of the main floor windows. However, cricket continues to thrive and Stoneleigh CC plays in the Cotswold Hills League against teams with evocative names like Long Itchington. Lord Leigh also owned an estate in Adlestrop, the village in Gloucestershire made famous by Edward Thomas's poem, and there is an annual fixture between the two villages for the Lord Leigh Cup.

The ground is unchanging in its charm and won the 2003 Wisden prize for the most beautiful ground in England. Perhaps its essence was best caught all those years ago in 1872 by John Lorraine Baldwin, writing as the game against I Zingari drew to its close: 'When all was finished there seemed a lingering desire on both sides not to leave the ground, as they gazed at the old Abbey calm and beautiful in its grandeur…'

Club captain Paul Lazenby stepped down from his role at the end of the 2019 season, having been captain since 1993. In his career he played more than 800 games, scored more than 24,000 runs and took more than 500 wickets.

Home to: Stoneleigh Cricket Club

Surnikovo Cricket Ground

Mežica, Slovenia

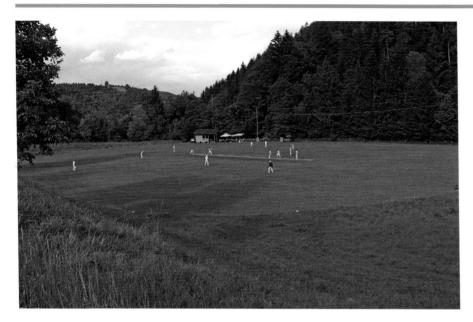

In 1974 a 13-year-old Slovenian lad, Borut Čegovnik, travelled to England on an extended visit to see his pen-pal in Kent and improve his English. The English friend was a keen cricketer, and it occurred to his father to give the young visitor some coaching so he wouldn't feel left out. Borut grew to like the game so much that when he returned home to Mežica, a small town in the Slovenian Alps near the Austrian border, he took a selection of cricket equipment and began to organise games.

Over the next few years he played predominantly single-wicket games with boys from the village. Then the group split up, many of them moving to the Slovenian capital, Ljubljana. A few years passed and interest had grown sufficiently among the expat community to form the Ljubljana Cricket Club. Mežica also developed a team, all of whose members were native Slovenians. Looking for somewhere to play, they found an ideal spot high up in the mountains.

A matting wicket was obtained and a small rudimentary pavilion created over the course of a couple of years. Some basic amenities such as a toilet were missing and it was sometimes more convenient to change al fresco. A nearby brook solved some of the other problems. One of the players volunteered to act as groundsman and a proper cricket ground emerged. Bit by bit, word spread about this idyllic haven and the ground began to attract touring parties from across Europe.

There was now so much interest in cricket in Slovenia that other clubs were set up, such as Maribor and Bela Krajina. A Slovenian national team was formed and played in the 2000 European Representative Championships for the first time, finishing fourth and going two places better in 2002. In 2004, 30 years after he first fell in love with the game, the initiator of Slovenian cricket, Borut Čegovnik, was still active enough to play for his country.

The spread of the game in recent years is very impressive. According to the ICC website, there are now two club sides in Ljubljana and two new clubs, Majšperk and Ptuj, in the north east. Even more remarkably, since 2003 more than 5,000 children have been taught cricket in junior schools throughout Slovenia. In 2009 cricket was introduced as a three-month module by the Faculty of Sport at the University of Ljubljana, in conjunction with the Slovenian Cricket Association. Nets have even been built in the grounds of one of the schools. And all because a Slovenian boy took a fancy to the game all those years ago.

Home to: Mežica Cricket Club

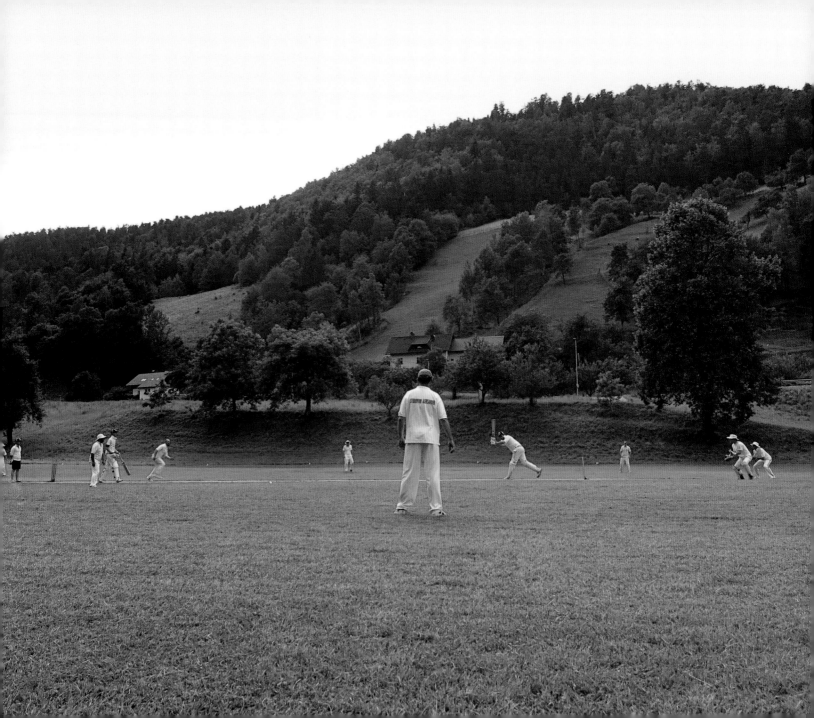

Sydney Cricket Ground

Sydney, Australia

Something about the SCG makes you feel that it hasn't gone quite as wholeheartedly futuristic as many other grounds. Certainly, it has modernised and expanded, pulled down and rebuilt to keep its Aussie Rules tenants and Big Bash franchise happy and its 48,000 capacity is not excessive in these days. But something of the character of the original cricket ground, which appealed to so many, appears to have been preserved.

That might have seemed improbable when it deliberately closed 'the Hill'. This broad expanse of banking at the south end of the ground was the favourite gathering place for working-class young men who sunned themselves while knocking back as many 'stubbies' as they could. Though it was probably the most famous and colourful spectator area in the whole of cricket, the administrators turned it into seating in the 1990s. But there was a nod to the past when the new stand was called Yabba's Hill. Yabba – Stephen Gascoigne (1878–1942) – was certainly the most famous barracker of all.

Many of the most frequently repeated and best-known classics are his. To a batsman adjusting his box: 'Those are the only balls you've touched all day!' To the English captain Douglas Jardine, as he brushed a fly away: 'Leave our flies alone, Jardine. They're the only friends you've got here.' To a slow batsman: 'Send 'im down a piano, see if 'e can play that!' Yabba was so integral to the experience of an Ashes series of that era that on his last tour of Australia, Jack Hobbs walked across to the Hill and shook his hand.

When Yabba's Hill was pulled down to make way for the new Victor Trumper Stand, SCG was still determined not to forget one of its most famous sons. A sculpture of Yabba was commissioned in characteristic barracking pose and allocated a seat in the ground in what must be a unique gesture to a spectator. As a rule, the Aussies don't do sentimental but this comes close.

Other features remain that date back closer to cricket's first association with the ground

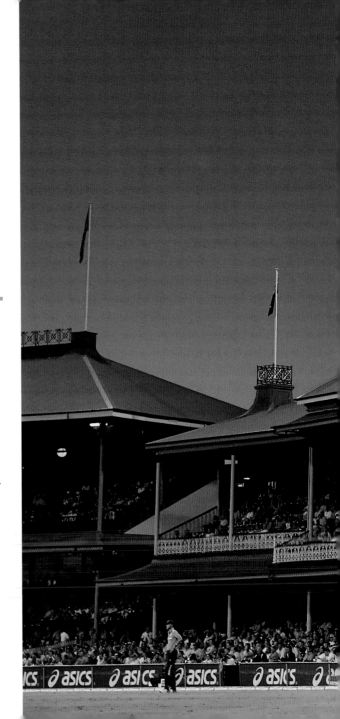

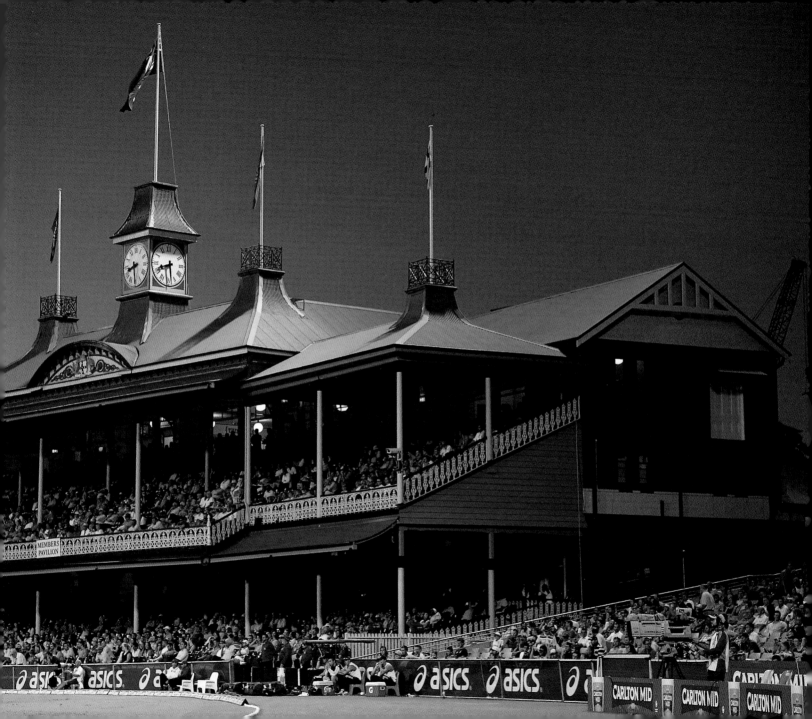

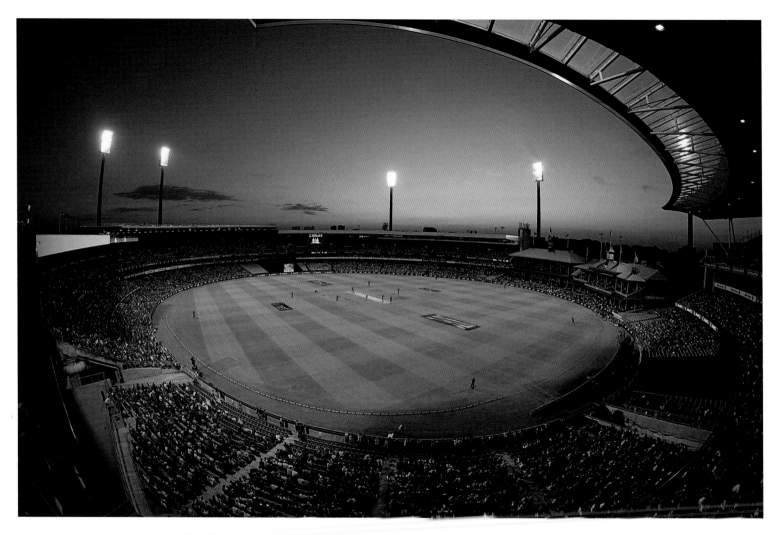

In the mid-19th century. In 1878 a Members' Pavilion was built, followed in 1896 by a Ladies' Pavilion. Spacious and green-roofed, their architecture fits in comfortably with the more modern stands and their future is protected by heritage listing. At the same time, a concrete cycling track was built which circled the inside of the ground, only of

interest because a carpenter involved with the construction happened to be George Bradman, father of 'the Don'. Boxer's Roller, the sandstone roller used around the turn of the 20th century, is also preserved. Boxer was the name of the horse who pulled the roller and he wore special shoes to avoid damaging the pitch. A similar roller is still

in use at Spout House, as a photograph elsewhere in the book shows, with seven-and-a-half men just about equal to the job that Boxer used to do.

While the ground has the reputation of being spinner-friendly, some of the batting here has been remarkable. In 1930 Bradman

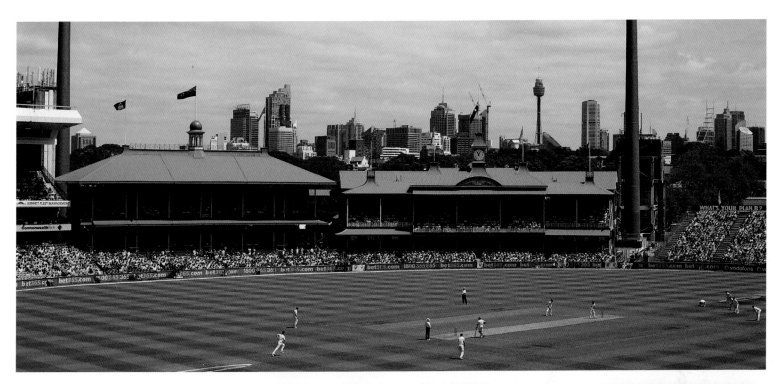

made his highest score of 452 not out against Queensland after scoring just three in the first innings; Brian Lara made 277 in 1993 and Michael Clarke scored 329 not out against India in 2012. A more sombre recollection is the sad death of Phillip Hughes during a match in November 2014. A plaque to his memory has been mounted at the ground and he has become part of the pantheon of SCG's notable cricketers.

Home to: New South Wales; Sydney Sixers

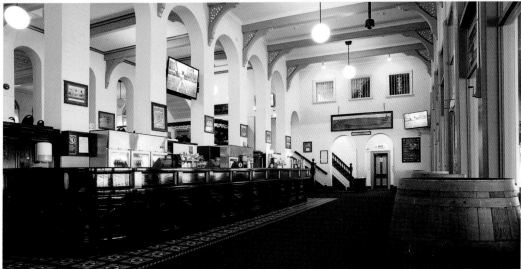

RIGHT: The cedar Long Bar in the heritage-listed Members' Pavilion is open to the public taking tours of the ground.

Valley of the Rocks

Lynton, Devon, England

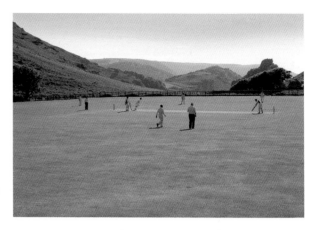

Lynton and Lynmouth CC say that they are probably more renowned for their playing venue than their cricketing achievements. As the club has only one team that plays in Division 3 of the North Devon League, their modesty may well be justified.

But any club who played here would probably feel the same, given the splendour of this location. The ground sits in the Valley of the Rocks, a uniquely beautiful area near the edge of Exmoor on the north coast of Devon and a favourite area for walkers. The dramatic rock formations are about 400 million years old.

The landscape appealed to the romantic imagination and Wordsworth and Coleridge were so struck by the locale that they started to write a story set in the area, although it was never completed. Part of R.D. Blackmore's famous romance *Lorna Doone* is also set in the valley.

The club was founded in 1876 and a ground was created by dint of a lot of rolling. Feral goats, badgers and foxes are common and the club has enclosed the playing area with a wire fence to keep them out, though not with total success. To earn a six, the ball has

to clear the 122-centimetre (4-foot) fence, not simply hit it on the full. Fielders are forever searching for balls lost in the gorse and heather. Like other seaside grounds, sea mists disrupt play. As in Bamburgh, gusts of wind sometimes blow over sight screens, so they are dispensed with.

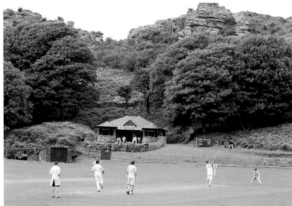

Set back in the shelter of trees is a beautiful pavilion of traditional stone construction. It is a faithful replica of the original, destroyed in an arson attack in 1999, and was rebuilt through the skills of a builder-member of the club. Unfortunately, all the records and many historic photos disappeared in the blaze.

However on the plus side, the club have a keen patron in Sir Christopher Ondaatje CBE, and local farmer and Chairman Robin May echoes the experience of Bude Cricket Club; their appearance in this book has led to increased enquiries from overseas touring teams. For a visiting batsman, compensation for an early dismissal is the opportunity to explore the stunning views within a short stroll of the ground.

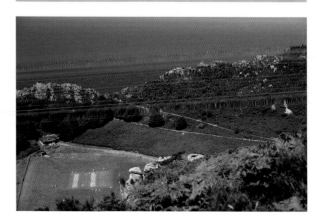

Home to: Lynton and Lynmouth Cricket Club

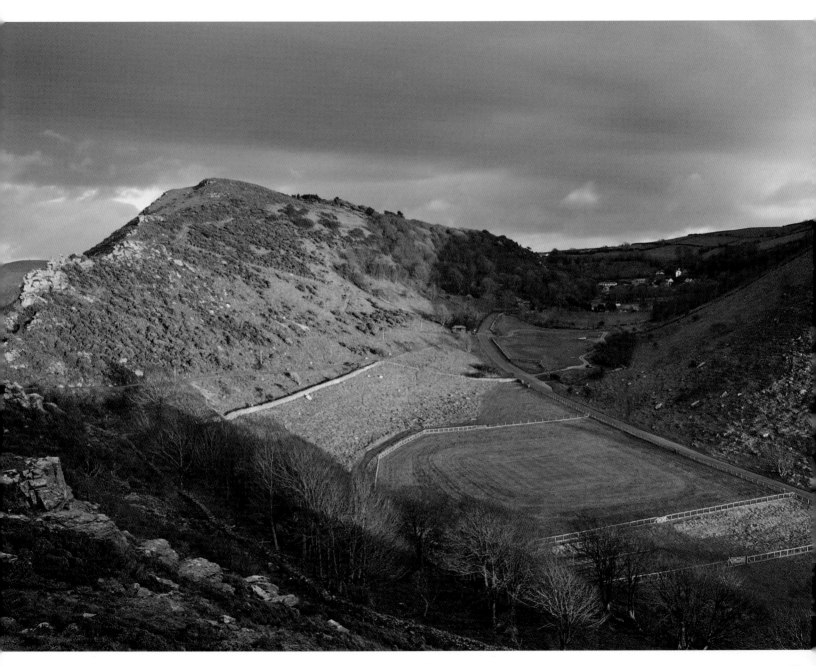

Vincent Square

Westminster School, London, England

As with a lot of ancient institutions, it is hard to put an exact date on the founding of Westminster School, but it is certainly one of the oldest schools in the country, dating back to the medieval monastery at Westminster Abbey in the 14th century. Henry VIII and Elizabeth I were both patrons of the school. The main buildings are situated in the heart of Westminster, close to Westminster Abbey and the Houses of Parliament. Former pupils include Ben Jonson, Edward Gibbon, Henry Purcell and Helena Bonham-Carter, but no first-class cricketers of any note.

Despite that, the school has its place in cricketing history, taking part in the first-ever schools match of which a record has been kept. The game took place at the Old Lord's Ground in Dorset Square in August 1794; the opponents were Charterhouse, and Westminster won by an innings and 102 runs. According to Geoff Tibballs in *No-balls and Googlies*, in those days schoolboy cricket wasn't encouraged by teachers because of 'the drunken horseplay' associated with the game. How different from today. It is said that the teams played under assumed names to avoid the wrath of the masters. That was probably just as well, because a

few years later when the headmaster of Eton discovered that his boys had arranged a secret cricket match with Westminster on Hounslow Heath, he flogged the entire team. The masters obviously came round to the idea as the Westminster team was very active throughout the whole of the 19th century, playing regularly against Eton, MCC, I Zingari and other sides.

The cricket ground, Vincent Square, is a relatively short walk from the school. It is an oasis of tree-sheltered green with a stylish pavilion dating from 1889 in the heart of the otherwise unrelenting urban environment. The school has added two hybrid wickets to increase playing times and there are plans to improve the drainage.

Cricket has been played here since the end of the 18th century, so its venerableness made it a very suitable place to stage a period-dress cricket match between a Wisden XI and an Authors' XI on the occasion of the 150th anniversary of *Wisden* in 2013 (shown right). The original Authors' XI, the Allahakbarries, was founded by J.M. Barrie in 1890 and writers such as P.G. Wodehouse, Rudyard Kipling, H.G. Wells, whose father

was a first-class cricketer, and A.A. Milne, a Westminster old boy, came to play for him. The modern Authors' XI included the former England cricketer, Ed Smith, and Sebastian Faulks, while Geoffrey Archer was an umpire. The match was a reminder of a time when there were many more parks like Vincent Square in the centre of London.

Home to: Westminster School

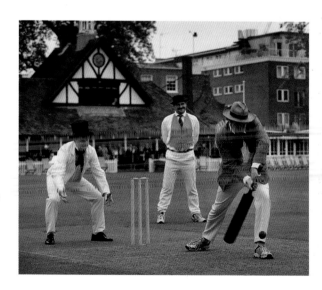

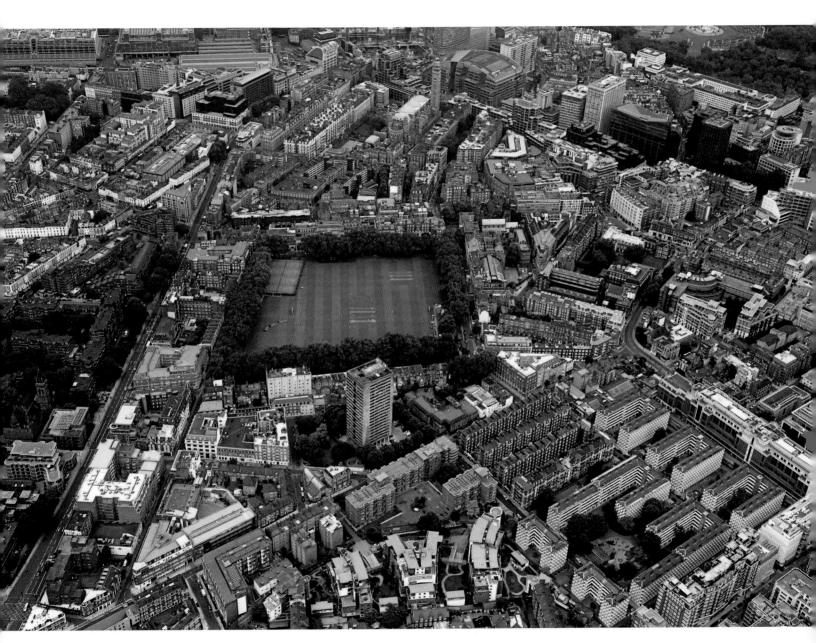

Wankhede Stadium

Mumbai, India

Wankhede Stadium, designed by Shashi Prabhu, was built in just under a year by the Mumbai Cricket Association after disputes arose over the allocation of tickets at the then main venue, Brabourne Stadium. The new ground opened in January 1975 and the first Test was a six-day series decider between India and West Indies. When Clive Lloyd of the West Indies reached his double century on the second day, a young man called Yogesh Maganlal Barot ran on to the pitch to shake his hand. A riot ensued, but diligent fans worked all night to clear up the damage and the match continued the next day. West Indies won the series 3–2.

The Wankhede Stadium was named after S.K. Wankhede, a politician and secretary of the Mumbai Cricket Association. Wankhede Stadium's main problem has been lack of space. It has only 13 acres whereas it could do with 20.

The stadium's capacity was 45,000 until major renovations and safety provisions reduced it to 33,108 in readiness for hosting the 2011 World Cup Final. The towering stands are named after Sunil Gavaskar, Vijay Merchant and Sachin Tendulkar. The north and south stands have 20 escalators, and the giant floodlights, erected in 1996, have helped to create an exciting atmosphere for day-night matches.

Wankhede was where Sachin Tendulkar fell in love with cricket after watching Sunil Gavaskar and Vivian Richards. Tendulkar was later part of India's 2011 World Cup Final win at the same stadium. In the 1979 Golden Jubilee match, England wicket-keeper Bob Taylor took 10 catches while Ian Botham scored 114 and took 13 wickets in England's 10-wicket victory against India. In 1985 Ravi Shastri hit six sixes in an over for Bombay against Baroda off the slow left arm spin bowling of Tilak Raj.

The circular stadium has also been the venue for international hockey, a 1980 double-wicket tournament (won by Ian Botham and Graham Gooch) and a public reception after India had beaten the West Indies to win the 1983 World Cup. Sachin played his final (200th) Test here in 2013 and scored 74.

Home to: Mumbai Cricket Team

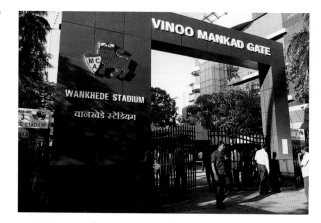

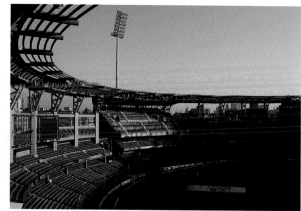

156

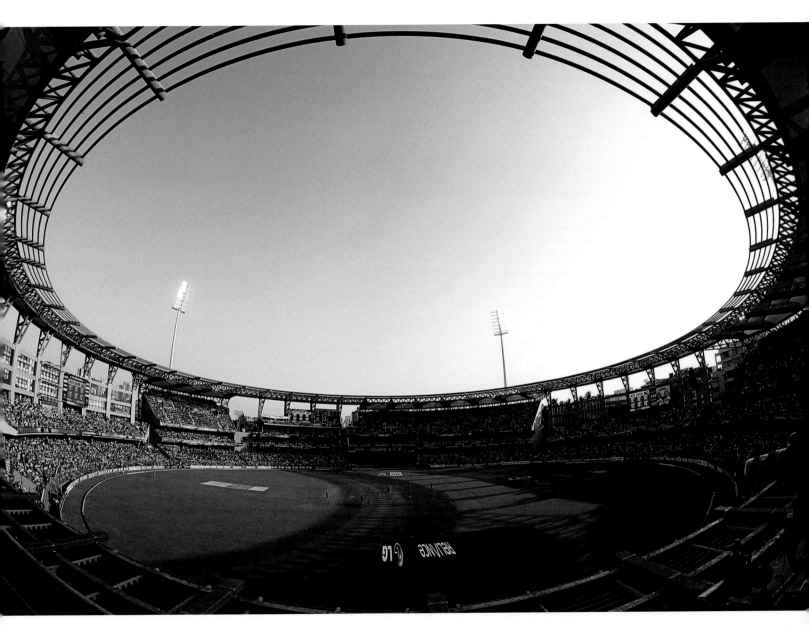

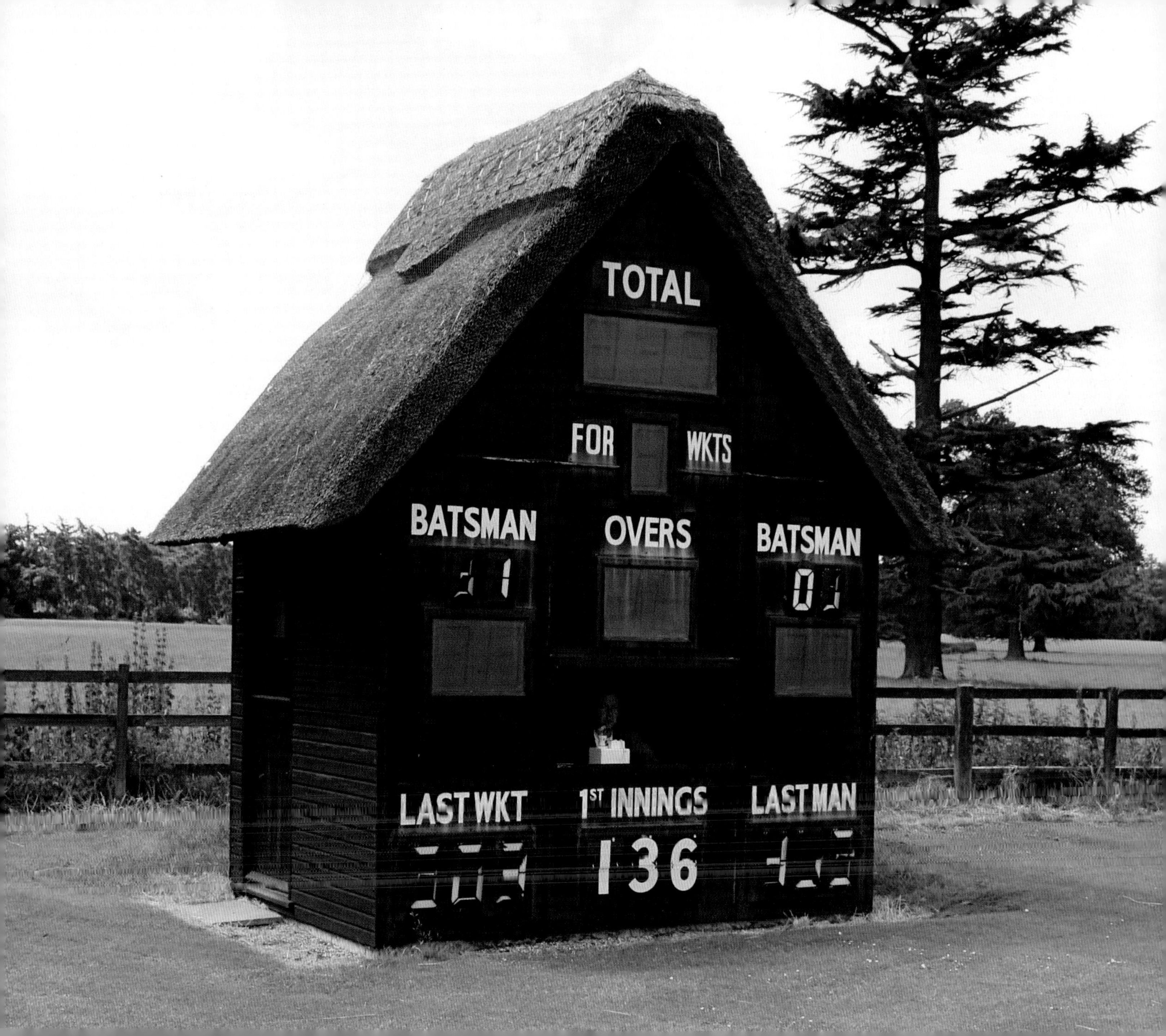
TOTAL
FOR
WKTS
BATSMAN
OVERS
BATSMAN
LAST WKT
1ST INNINGS
LAST MAN
136

Whitbread Estate

Southill, Bedfordshire, England

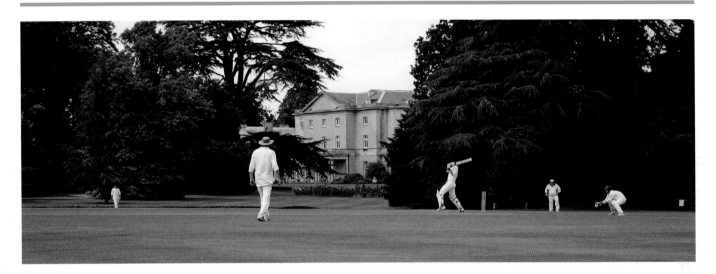

Southill Park Cricket Club has been playing in the picturesque setting of the Whitbread Estate in the village of Southill near Biggleswade since 1884, or maybe even earlier. Local journals from the 1840s refer to 'a large open space' in the park, where archery tournaments were sometimes held on the same grounds that cricket was played, and, two or three times during the season, matches were fixed 'between members of the house staff – butlers, coachmen, gardeners, stable boys against eleven of the village yokels'.

Southill House, with its acres of beautiful manicured parkland and wooded grounds, has been the ancestral home of the famous Whitbread brewing family for hundreds of years. The house contains some historic English paintings by Sir Joshua Reynolds and Thomas Gainsborough. A member of the family is always club president and there is a good deal of cricketing interaction between the estate, the club and the villagers, including Wednesday games between the estate workers and local businesses, schools and other organisations. The estate also generously carries out a significant amount of repair and maintenance work on the ground and buildings.

The club calls itself 'small' but still manages to run 10 teams. Even though Southill Park is in Bedfordshire, the Saturday side plays in the Whiting & Partners Cambs and Hunts Premier League, returning to the Bedfordshire County Premier League on Sundays. The club is particularly proud of its U-15s, which in 2014 secured a place in the Group Final, described as 'the biggest day in the club's history'.

Eye-catching are two magnificent protected cedars within the playing area, worth four if they're hit; also instantly attractive are the pavilion and scorer's box, both thatched. The recently refurbished 100-year-old pavilion won a Sport England award for pavilion improvements. The scorebox is particularly lovely and would not look out of place in a production of Hansel and Gretel. Surprisingly, it is a mere 25 years old. With such stylish surroundings, it is small wonder that the ground has been frequently used to host county finals and representative games.

Home to: Southill Park Cricket Club

Close of Play – Author's Note

The thought of writing about grounds you have never seen or are likely to is a bit daunting. Someone actually suggested I visit them all. It was a good joke and, budget and timeframe aside, a lovely idea.

Of all the grounds in this book, I confess to having watched cricket at only six. But I have seen some of the others on television; Cheltenham College I could very easily imagine because it was a mid-19th-century establishment similar to the school I attended. A much younger me had also played cricket at some beautiful English village grounds. So a chunk of the foundation was in place.

Work on each new venue began with the stunning photographs in this book. Sometimes it was the design that took my attention, sometimes the location. If the design, I tried to find out more about the architect's brief and was often pointed in the right direction by Matthew Levison, himself a professional designer. For one ground, he highlighted that the main stand had been designed to resemble a cricket cap - something I wouldn't have noticed myself and wasn't totally convinced by when I looked closer.

Although Wikipedia and ESPNcricinfo were useful as a rule, I was wary about the Internet in general. It could be helpful but also wildly varying in, say, crowd capacities. The best kind of information came from newspaper articles written by knowledgeable journalists and writers such as Mike Amos of the *Northern Echo* and Fabian Muir writing from Berlin.

While establishing a venue's name should be straightforward, in these days of naming rights it isn't. Some have had many sponsors and the name has changed frequently, out-dating it very quickly. I tended to go with what I think the public calls a ground. However, I don't claim 100 per cent consistency. For instance, I think it is generally agreed that the Oval is the one in Kennington, London. Just the same, I call it the Kia Oval because its sponsorship is well established and to identify it from the many other Ovals.

Almost every ground has what marketing men call a USP (Unique Selling Point) - the feature which differentiates it from every other. In Dharamshala it is the amazing location which is overlooked by the Himalayas. In Chail, it was a helipad and in Queenstown, New Zealand, planes taking off from the nearby airport, which fly immediately behind the bowler's arm. In Muzaffarabad, Pakistan, the Narol stadium had been destroyed by an earthquake; in Wellington, the Basin Reserve had been created by one. The Oval Maidan in Mumbai was built on land reclaimed from the sea. One or two stories particularly caught my attention. Heading the list are the two William Ainsleys, grandfather and grandson. Between them, they were the club secretary of Spout House near Bilsdale in North

Yorkshire in one unbroken span from 1874 to 2012. Close behind came the incident when Jack Hobbs, playing at Sydney on his last tour of Australia in 1928–29, strode across the ground to shake the hand of the barracking scourge of the English Test team, Yabba. Nor was I expecting to find organised cricket in Slovenia and Corfu. Their stories are worth reading.

Other general impressions were the beauty of the New Zealand grounds, the number of English village sides associated with stately homes and the amount of amiable patronage the local teams received. For sheer strangeness, little beat the Goldfield Ashes played at Charters Towers in Queensland, St Moritz CC playing on the frozen lake and Mitcham CC with its pitch and pavilion separated by a main road. By the time I had finished, the individual grounds had developed personalities and were easily identifiable. I hope it's the same for you. Ironically, I missed seeing the whole of the 2016 Twenty20 World Cup - with many of the games taking place in locations in this book - in order to write a book about cricket.

Finally, I might have thought twice about writing this book if I had realised how few synonyms there are for ground, stadium and venue. I did my best to ration myself to using them no more than once a paragraph.

Brian Levison,
Oxford

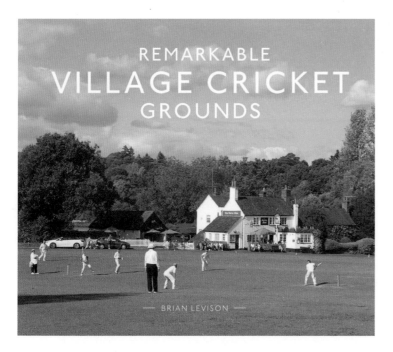

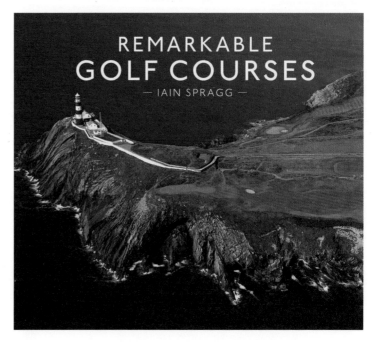

Remarkable Village Cricket Grounds (224 pages)
by Brian Levison • ISBN: 978-1-911595-56-4

Featuring: Abbotsbury, Abinger Hammer, Aldborough, Alderley Edge, Ambleside, Arthington, Audley End, Bearsted, Belvoir Castle, Benenden Green, Bilsington, Blenheim Palace, Booth, Bridgetown, Bude, Burnsall, Castleton, Chagford, Cholmondeley Castle, Clanfield, Clumber Park, Cockington, Coldharbour, Coniston, Copley, Cowdray Park, Crickhowell, Doo'cot Park, Dumbleton, Ebernoe, Elmley Castle, Firle, Fulking, Goodwood, Grassington, Great Budworth, Hagley Hall, Haworth, Holkham Hall, Honley, Hovingham, Ickwell, Instow, Keswick, Kildale, Kinross, Knightshayes Court, Knole Park, Leigh, Linkenholt, Longparish, Luddenfoot, Lurgashall, Lustleigh, Lyndhurst, Marchwiel, Menai Bridge, Meopham, Mountnessing, Mytholmroyd, Nettlebed, North Nibley, Northop, Old Town, Oxted, Patterdale, Penshurst Place, Raby Castle, Ramsbottom, Rawtenstall, Saltaire, Sedgewick, Sheepscombe, Shobrooke Park, Sicklinghall, Sidmouth, Snettisham, Southborough, Southill Park, Spout House, Stanton, Stanway, Stoneleigh, Tilford, Triangle, Ullenwood, Uplyme, Valley of the Rocks, Warborough, Warkworth Castle, White Coppice, Wingfield, Winnington Park

Remarkable Golf Courses (224 pages)
by Iain Spragg. • ISBN: 978-1-911595-04-5

Featuring: Abu Dhabi, The Addington, Ailsa Championship Course, Arikikapakapa, Arrowhead Golf Club, Augusta National, Barnbougle, Barra, The Brabazon, Brocket Hall, Cape Kidnappers, Carnoustie, Machrihanish, Royal County Down, Chicago Golf Club, The Church Course, Clearview Golf Club, Alcanada, Coeur d'Alene Resort, Cypress Point, The Dunes Golf Resort, Fuego Maya, Furnace Creek, Green Monkey Golf Course, Harbour Town Links, The Isle of Harris, Icelandic Golf, Ile Aux Cerfs, Jack's Point, Jade Dragon Snow Mountain, Ko'olau Golf Club, Kobe Golf Club, La Paz, Leaders Peak Golf Club, Leeds Castle, The Lodhi, Lofoten Links, Lost City Golf Course, Llanymynech, Lundin Ladies, Majlis Course, Manele Golf Course, Merapi Golf, Mission Hills Resort, Moor Park, Naldehra Golf Club, Oakmont Country Club, The Ocean Course, Musselburgh, Royal Troon, The Old Course, St Andrews, Old Head (cover), Painswick, Pebble Beach, Pennard, Pine Valley, Prestwick, Punta Mita Pacifico, Real Club Valderrama, The Rise, Royal Melbourne, Royal North Devon, RTJ Golf Club, Rye Golf Club, Sedona, Seven Canyons Club, The Severiano Ballesteros Course, Bro Hof Slott, Stadium Course, PGA Catalunya Resort, Stadium Course, TPC Sawgrass, Stoke Park, The Straits, Streamsong Red, Streamsong Blue, Torrey Pines Golf Club, Tralee Golf Club, Tromsø Golf Club, Upper Course, Ushuaia Golf Club, Victoria National, West Links, West Course, Wolf Creek